YOUR ROAD MAP FOR SUCCESS WORKBOOK

JOHN MAXWELL

THOMAS NELSON PUBLISHERS®
Nashville

A Division of Thomas Nelson, Inc.
www.ThomasNelson.com

Published in Nashville, Tennessee, by Thomas Nelson, Inc.

Unless otherwise noted, Scripture quotations are from the HOLY BIBLE: NEW INTER-NATIONAL VERSION®. Copyright © 1973, 1978, 1984 by International Bible Society. Used by permission of Zondervan Publishing House. All rights reserved.

Scripture quotations noted KJV are from the KING JAMES VERSION.

ISBN 0-7852-6575-9

Printed in the United States of America

02 03 04 05 VG 6 5 4 3 2 1

CONTENTS

INTRODUCTION

Whit Hobbs wrote, "Success is waking up in the morning, whoever you are, wherever you are, however old or young, and bounding out of bed because there's something out there that you love to do, that you believe in, that you're good at—something that's bigger than you are, and you can hardly wait to get at it again today."

The success journey will not look the same for everyone because the picture of success is different for every person. But the principles used to take the journey are constant. It doesn't matter where you are now. You can be successful, beginning today.

My desire in this workbook is to provide the principles and action steps necessary for your success journey. I want to help you discover your personal Road Map for Success, teach you what it means to be on the success journey, answer many of your questions, and equip you with what you'll need to improve yourself and keep growing. In the process, you'll discover that success is for everyone: the homemaker and the businessperson, the student and the retiree, the athlete and the local church pastor, the factory worker and the entrepreneur. Turn the page, and let's start the journey together.

Week

1

WHAT IS SUCCESS?

DAY 1
The Journey Is More Fun When You Know Where You're Going

DAY 2
The Traditional Picture of Success

DAY 3
The Right Picture of Success

DAY 4
Potential and Investment

DAY 5
Take the Journey

PRINCIPAL QUESTIONS

DAY 1: How do I make decisions?

DAY 2: How do I define success?

DAY 3: What is my purpose?

DAY 4: What am I doing to grow toward my potential and invest in others?

DAY 5: Am I leading my own journey, or following someone else's path?

THE JOURNEY IS MORE FUN
WHEN YOU KNOW WHERE YOU'RE GOING

Several years ago, as I was thumbing through *Success* magazine, I came across a study that Gallup did on what people thought it meant to be a success. That appealed to me because I've always been interested in helping others to become successful, and I wanted to know what Gallup had gleaned. Their answers fell into twelve categories, but the number one answer was "good health." Fifty-eight percent of the people identified that with success over anything else. I don't know about you, but I value good health—and after my heart attack I value it even more. But if I had only good health and nothing else, I don't know that I would label myself "successful."

I've discovered that people often find it hard to define success. But if you don't know what success is, how will you ever achieve it? That's why I want to help you identify a definition of success that will work for you.

Let me begin this week by telling you a story. A few years ago, I stood before the seventy-four employees of INJOY—the organization I founded in 1985—and prepared to tell them some news that I knew would be exciting to some and discouraging to others. I was going to tell them that in a year's time, we would be moving the company from San Diego, California, to Atlanta, Georgia.

My friend Dick Peterson, INJOY's president at the time, and I had been talking about the possibility of moving the company for about six months. It had begun as a casual "what if . . ." conversation, but then we started giving it more serious thought. We weighed the advantages and asked our director of finance to run some numbers. We talked about the opportunities that such a move would bring. And finally, we determined that moving to Atlanta made sense professionally, logistically, and economically. We knew that if we wanted to go to a new level in our growth and development, not only as a company but also as individuals, we needed to make the change.

As we made the announcement, our concern was for the people on the INJOY team, and I saw a whole range of reactions to the news. Some looked shocked. Others looked as if they had been punched in the stomach. From our managers I saw relief: they had been keeping their knowledge of the move secret for weeks.

For fifty minutes, Dick Peterson and I explained all of our reasons for the move, gave them stats and information on Atlanta, and showed them a video from the Atlanta Chamber of Commerce. And we told them that anyone who was willing to go to Atlanta would have a job when he or she got there. Then we introduced two people who had flown in from Atlanta's top real-estate agency to answer questions.

We weren't sure what kind of reaction we would get from our staff. We were proposing a major move that would radically change their lives. What a surprise it was when more than 90 percent of the team said they would move or at least consider moving to Atlanta! They were willing to take the trip.

What would it take for you to pick up and move to a new city?

Great job opportunity; chance to see new things and experience new things; would need to "feel right"

How do we make choices? What factors into our daily and big-picture decisions? A majority of the time it's the idea that where we are going is going to be better than where we are right now. There has to be a reward for taking the chance or making the trip.

How does a recent decision you've made relate to the desire to be successful?

Redoubling my efforts at work; I want my contribution to help our office get results

TAKE ACTION

Ask three people to define success. It's best if you can do this one-on-one rather than in a group setting. I suggest asking people with different roles—one person could be your boss or a coworker, another could be a friend, and another could be a relative. Jot down a few notes about each person's ideas about success. Look at how their responses are similar and how they differ. Finally, write out your own definition of success based on your experiences, relationships, and other influences.

SUCCESS IS

_____

_____

_____

Lori - stable/happy home ; healthy marriage ;
rewarding career ; financially stable

THE TRADITIONAL PICTURE OF SUCCESS

I believe that we make many of our decisions because we are striving to be successful. Each of us has a picture in mind of what we want our career to look like, our family to look like, and yes, from an early age we often conjure up images of the houses, cars, and things we would like to obtain. In many persons' minds, success is something way off in the distance that they will run themselves ragged to get to—if they ever get to it.

The problem for most people who want to be successful is *not* that they can't achieve success. The main obstacle for them is that they misunderstand success. Maltbie D. Babcock said, "One of the most common mistakes and one of the costliest is thinking that success is due to some genius, some magic, something or other which we do not possess."

What does success look like?

Spiritual, mental, physical, relational growth

What would you be able to do as a successful person?

Influence others to be more successful

Most people have a vague picture of what it means to be a successful person. It looks something like this:

the wealth of Bill Gates
the physique of Arnold Schwarzenegger
(or Cindy Crawford)

the intelligence of Albert Einstein

the athletic ability of Michael Jordan

the business prowess of Donald Trump

the social grace and poise of Jackie Kennedy

the imagination of Walt Disney

the heart of Mother Teresa

That sounds absurd, but it's closer to the truth than we would like to admit.

> *Describe a time when you tried to act, dress, or talk like someone else. How did people respond to you? How did you feel about yourself? How long did you keep up the facade?*
>
> Parachute pants in High School ?!?! I looked and felt stupid!

Many of us picture success as being like someone else—or more likely, like a number of other people. But it's not reasonable to think we can be exactly like someone else, and more important than that, you shouldn't want to be! If you tried to become just like even one of these other people, you wouldn't be successful. You would be a bad imitation of your hero, and you would eliminate the possibility of becoming the person you were meant to be.

THE WRONG PICTURE OF SUCCESS

Even if you avoid the trap of thinking that success means being like some other person, you might still have a wrong picture of success. Frankly, the majority of people misunderstand it. They wrongly equate it with achievement of some sort, with arriving at a destination or attaining a goal. Here are several of the most common misconceptions about success:

Wealth

How much money does a successful person have? plenty

Probably the most common misunderstanding about success is that it's the same as having money. A lot of people believe that if they accumulate wealth, they will be successful. But wealth does not bring contentment or success.

Industrialist John D. Rockefeller, a man so rich that he gave away more than $350 million in his lifetime, was once asked how much money it would take to satisfy him. His reply: "Just a little bit more." King Solomon of ancient Israel, said to be not only the wisest but also the richest man who ever lived, asserted, "Whoever loves money never has money enough; / whoever loves wealth is never satisfied with his income."[1]

Money doesn't guard a person from challenges or problems. Wealth and what it brings are, at best, fleeting. In 1923, a small group of the world's wealthiest men met at the Edgewater Beach Hotel in Chicago, Illinois. They were a Who's Who of wealth and power. At that time, they controlled more money than the total amount contained in the United States Treasury. Here is a list of who was there and what eventually happened to them:

- CHARLES SCHWAB—president of the largest independent steel company—died broke.

- ARTHUR CUTTEN—greatest of the wheat speculators—died abroad, insolvent.

- RICHARD WHITNEY—president of the New York Stock Exchange—died just after release from Sing Sing prison.

- ALBERT FALL—member of a U.S. president's cabinet—was pardoned from prison so that he could die at home.

- JESS LIVERMORE—greatest "bear" on Wall Street—committed suicide.

- LEON FRASER—president of the Bank of International Settlements—committed suicide.

- IVAR KREUGER—head of the world's greatest monopoly—committed suicide.[2]

Give your own example of a person who had plenty of money, but also a number of problems.

Aunts & Uncles

Greek millionaire Aristotle Onassis, who retained his wealth and died at a ripe old age, recognized that money isn't the same as success. He maintained, "After you reach a certain point, money becomes unimportant. What matters is success."

How much emphasis have you placed on money when it comes to defining success?

| 1 | 2 | 3 | 4 | ⑤ | 6 | 7 | 8 | 9 | 10 |

little _____ a great deal

A SPECIAL FEELING

What does success feel like? exhilirating

Another common misconception is that people have achieved success when they feel successful or happy. But trying to *feel* successful is probably even more difficult than trying to become wealthy. Look at real-estate developer Donald Trump, for example. He said, "The real measure of success is how happy you are. I have a lot of friends who don't have a lot of money, but they are a lot happier than I am, so therefore I say that they are probably more successful." Trump, whom many consider successful, believes that happiness is success. Maybe his happy friends think *he* is the successful one. This belief demonstrates that many people equate success with what they don't have.

Complete the following sentence:
If I had __a Nobel prize?__, I would be successful.

The continual search for happiness is a primary reason that so many people are miserable. If you make happiness your goal, you are almost certainly destined to fail. You will be on a continual roller coaster, changing from successful to unsuccessful with every mood change. Life is uncertain, and emotions aren't stable. Happiness simply cannot be relied upon as a measure of success.

How much emphasis have you placed on feeling happy when it comes to defining success?

1	2	3	4	5	6	(7)	8	9	10

little_____ a great deal

SPECIFIC AND WORTHWHILE POSSESSIONS

Successful people own: __convertibles.__

Think back to when you were a kid. Chances are there was a time when you wanted something intensely, and you believed that if you possessed that thing, it would make a significant difference in your life.

List the one thing that you just had to have as a child:_____

For me, it was a burgundy-and-silver Schwinn bicycle. When I was nine years old, the thing to do in our neighborhood was to race around on our bikes. We had short races to see who was the fastest; we made ramps out of plywood to see who could jump the farthest; and on some Saturdays we mapped out a cross-country course that took us halfway across town and back.

Back then I was riding an old hand-me-down bicycle that had belonged to my brother, Larry, and I had trouble keeping up with some of the kids on newer bikes. But I figured that if I had that new Schwinn bike, I would have it made. I would have the newest, fastest, best-looking bike among all my friends, and I would make them all eat my dust.

On Christmas morning that year, when I looked under the tree, I saw my vision of what a bicycle ought to be. It had mud flaps, chrome, bells, lights—the works. For a while it was great. I loved that bike, and I spent a lot of time riding it. But I soon discovered that it didn't bring me the success or long-term contentment that I hoped for and expected.

> *The item you listed above—the one you had to have as a child—do you still have it? Take a moment to think about all the "must have" items that we throw out, sell at garage sales, trade in, or upgrade every few years.*

The process of discovering that a certain item wouldn't bring me lasting happiness or success has repeated itself in my life. I found that success didn't come when I became a starter on my high-school basketball team, when I became the student-body president in college, or when I bought my first house. It has never come as the result of possessing something I wanted. Possessions are, at best, a temporary fix. Success cannot be attained or measured that way.

> *How much emphasis have you placed on possessions when it comes to defining success?*
>
> 1   2   ③   4   5   6   7   8   9   10
>
> little _____ a great deal

POWER

> *A successful person usually has* __25+__ *(number) followers.*

Charles McElroy once joked, "Power is usually recognized as an excellent short-term antidepressant." That statement contains a lot of truth because power often gives the appearance of success, but even then, it's only temporary.

You've probably heard before the quote from English historian Lord Acton: "Power tends to corrupt and absolute power corrupts absolutely." Abraham Lincoln echoed that belief when he said, "Nearly all men can stand adversity, but if you want to test a man's character, give him power." Power really is a test of character.

Name a person who has used his power to benefit others: Popes

Name a person who has used his power to harm others: Hitler

In the hands of a person of integrity, it is of tremendous benefit; in the hands of a tyrant, it causes terrible destruction. By itself, power is neither positive nor negative. And it is not the source of security or success. Besides, all dictators—even benevolent ones—eventually lose power.

How much emphasis have you placed on power when it comes to defining success?

1   2   3   4   5   6   (7)   8   9   10

little _____ a great deal

ACHIEVEMENT

A successful person has achieved: their goals

Many people have what I call "destination disease." They believe that if they can arrive somewhere—attain a position, accomplish a goal, or have a relationship with the right person—they will be successful.

What position (career, marriage, status, etc.) did you once aspire to that you are now in? Consultant

Do you consider yourself successful because of that position? no

At one time, I viewed success as a place where I would arrive. I defined it as the progressive realization of a predetermined, worthwhile goal. But over time I realized that the definition fell short of the mark.

Simply achieving goals doesn't guarantee success or contentment. Look at what happened with Michael Jordan. A few years ago, he decided to retire from basketball, saying that he had accomplished all the goals he had wanted to achieve. And then he went on to play baseball in the minor leagues—but not for long. He couldn't stay away from the game of basketball. Playing the game, being in the midst of the process, was the thing. You see, success isn't a list of goals to be checked off one after another. It's not reaching a destination. *Success is a journey.*

Rewrite your definition of success without including references to wealth, feelings, possessions, power, or achievement.

_____

_____

_____

How does your success statement reflect the idea that success is a journey?

_____

_____

_____

TAKE ACTION

Read a short biography on the life of a past leader—political, religious, or business—and try to identify how he defined succes. How did he reflect this view in his decisions and actions? Did his definition reflect any of the misconceptions listed in today's lesson? Did his definition of success ever change during his time of leadership? Was this person ultimately successful?

The Right Picture of Success

So what does it take to be a success? Two things are required: the right picture of success and the right principles for getting there.

The picture of success isn't the same for any two people because we're all created as unique individuals. But the process is the same for everyone. It's based on principles that do not change. After more than twenty-five years of knowing successful people and studying the subject, I have developed the following definition of success:

Success is . . .

> *knowing your purpose in life,*
> *growing to reach your maximum potential, and*
> *sowing seeds that benefit others.*

How is this definition of success different from your own?

_____

_____

_____

This definition is based on the idea that success is a journey rather than a destination. And no matter how long you live or what you decide to do in life, you will never exhaust your capacity to grow toward your potential or run out of opportunities to help others. When you see success as a journey, you'll never have the problem of trying to "arrive" at an elusive, final destination. And you'll never find yourself in a position where you have accomplished some ultimate goal, only to discover that you're still unfulfilled and searching for something else to do.

Can you think of a time in your life when you thought, Finally, I've made it, *only to discover that there was a whole new set of challenges awaiting you?*

_____

_____

_____

Another benefit of focusing on the journey of success instead of on arriving at a destination or achieving a goal is that you have the potential to become a success *today*. The very moment that you redefine success as finding your purpose, growing to your potential, and helping others, successful is something you *are right now*, not something you vaguely hope one day to be.

To get a better handle on these aspects of success, let's take a look at each one of them. Today we'll start with purpose, and tomorrow we'll pick up with potential and investing in others.

KNOWING YOUR PURPOSE

Nothing can take the place of knowing your purpose. Millionaire industrialist Henry J. Kaiser, the founder of Kaiser Aluminum as well as the Kaiser-Permanente health care system, said, "The evidence is overwhelming that you cannot begin to achieve your best unless you set some aim in life." Or put another way, if you don't try actively to discover your purpose, you're likely to spend your life doing the wrong things.

Write out two or three things you hope to accomplish in your life.

_____

_____

_____

I believe that God created every person for a purpose. According to psychologist Viktor Frankl, "Everyone has his own specific vocation or mission in life. Everyone must carry out a concrete assignment that demands fulfillment. Therein he cannot be replaced, nor can his life be repeated. Thus everyone's task is as unique as his specific opportunity to implement it." Each of us has a purpose for which we were created. Our responsibility—and our greatest joy—is to identify it.

Here are some questions to ask yourself to help you identify your purpose:

What am I searching for?

_____

_____

_____

All of us have a strong desire buried in our hearts, something that speaks to our deepest thoughts and feelings, something that sets our souls on fire. Some people have a strong sense of what that is when they're just children. Others take half a lifetime to discover it. But no matter what, it's there. You need only to find it.

Why was I created? What are my unique gifts and talents?

_____

_____

_____

Each of us is different. No one else in the world has exactly the same gifts, talents, background, or future as you do. That's one of the reasons it would be a serious mistake for you to try to be someone other than yourself.

Think about your unique mix of abilities, the resources available to you, your personal history, and the opportunities around you. If you objectively identify these factors and discover the desire of your heart, you will have made a lot of progress toward discovering your purpose in life.

*Do I believe in my potential? How do I reflect this confidence or lack of
confidence in my everyday activities?*

_____

_____

_____

You cannot consistently act in a manner inconsistent with the way you
see yourself. If you don't believe that you have potential, you will never
try to reach it. And if you aren't willing to work toward reaching your
potential, you will never be successful.

   You should take the advice of President Theodore Roosevelt, who
said, "Do what you can, with what you have, where you are." If you do
that with your eyes fixed on your life purpose, then that is all that anyone can expect of you.

When do I start my success journey? What am I waiting on?

_____

_____

_____

Some people live their lives from day to day, allowing others to dictate
what they do and how they do it. They never try to discover their true purpose for living. Others know their purpose, yet never act on it. They're
waiting for inspiration or permission or an invitation to get started. But if
they wait much longer, they'll never get going. So the answer to the question "When do I start?" is *now.*

*How can you resolve today to start on your success journey? What will
need to change in your attitude and actions?*

_____

_____

_____

TAKE ACTION

Review today's questions and reflect on your purpose. What were you created to do? How do your unique gifts and talents affirm this purpose? Talk to a close friend and receive feedback on what he sees as your greatest gifts and talents. Brainstorm together about ways you can live out your purpose. Should you be volunteerinjg or possibly looking at different careers? Or maybe your conversation confirms that you are already on the right course. That is just as valuable!

DAY 4

POTENTIAL AND INVESTMENT

You have started your success journey! You have found your purpose, and today we are going to look at ways to continue growing to your potential and ways you can help others.

GROWING TO YOUR POTENTIAL

Novelist H. G. Wells held that wealth, notoriety, place, and power are no measures of success whatsoever. The only true measure of success is the ratio between what we might have been and what we have become. In other words, success comes as the result of growing to our potential.

It's been said that our potential is God's gift to us, and what we do with it is our gift to Him. But at the same time, our potential is probably our greatest untapped resource. Henry Ford observed, "There is no man living who isn't capable of doing more than he thinks he can do."

In your own words, describe why people fall short of their potential.

_____

_____

_____

We have nearly limitless potential, yet too few ever try to reach it. Why? The answer lies in this: We can do *anything*, but we can't do *everything*. Many people let everyone around them decide their agenda in life. As a result, they never really dedicate themselves to *their* purpose in life. They become a jack-of-all-trades, master of none—rather than a jack-of-few-trades, focused on one.

What is your initial thought when it comes to trying something new? (Check one)

❑ *I have to be the best.*

❑ *I'll give it my best.*

❑ *It doesn't really matter how I do. I'll never be the best at it.*

If always having to be the best or not even trying because you know you'll never be the best describes you more than you'd like, you're probably ready to take steps to make a change. Here are four principles to put you on the road to growing toward your potential.

1. CONCENTRATE ON ONE MAIN GOAL

Nobody ever reached her potential by scattering herself in twenty directions. Reaching your potential requires focus. That's why it's so important for you to discover your purpose. Once you've decided where to focus your attention, you must decide what you are willing to give up to do it. And that's crucial. There can be no success without sacrifice. The two go hand in hand. If you desire to accomplish little, sacrifice little. But if you want to accomplish great things, be willing to sacrifice much.

Write out your purpose statement.

_____

_____

_____

Now list at least three things that you will have to give up in order to fulfill your purpose. What do you need to sacrifice?

_____

_____

_____

2. CONCENTRATE ON CONTINUAL IMPROVEMENT

David D. Glass, chief executive officer of Wal-Mart stores, was once asked whom he admired most. His answer was Wal-Mart founder Sam Walton. He remarked, "There's never been a day in his life, since I've known him, that he didn't improve in some way."

Commitment to continual improvement is the key to reaching your potential and to being successful. Each day you can become a little bit better than you were yesterday. It puts you one step closer to your potential. And you'll also find that what you *get* as the result of your growth is not nearly as important as what you *become* along the way.

By answering the following questions, you should be able to make a list of things to do each day that will help you grow to your potential.

Whom should you talk with or learn from?

_____

What books, newspapers, or magazines should you read?

_____

What activities should you participate in? (exercise, volunteer work, team sports)

_____

How can other media help you grow? (TV programs, the Internet, audio lessons, etc.)

_____

3. FORGET THE PAST

My friend Jack Hayford, pastor of Church on the Way in Van Nuys, California, commented, "The past is a dead issue, and we can't gain any momentum moving toward tomorrow if we are dragging the past behind us." Unfortunately, that's what too many people do: they drag the past with them wherever they go. And as a result, they never make any progress.

I like the attitude of Cyrus Curtis, who once owned the *Saturday Evening Post*. He had a sign hanging in his office that announced, "Yesterday ended last night." It was his way of reminding himself and his employees that the past is done, and they should be looking forward, not back.

What from your past has the potential to hold you back?

_____

_____

_____

Maybe you've made a lot of mistakes in your life, or you've had an especially difficult past with many obstacles. Work your way through it and move on. Don't let it prevent you from reaching your potential.

What steps can you take to resolve past issues? (righting a wrong, talking to someone, letting go of a past pain)

_____

_____

_____

If you need inspiration, think of other people who overcame seemingly insurmountable obstacles, such as Booker T. Washington. He was born into slavery and was denied access to the resources available to white society, but he never let that prevent him from pursuing his potential. He founded the Tuskegee Institute and the National Black Business League. He said, "I have learned that success is to be measured not so much by the position that one has reached in life as by the obstacles which one has overcome while trying to succeed."

Think of Franklin Delano Roosevelt. In 1921, at the age of thirty-nine, he had a severe case of polio, which left him disabled and in terrible pain. He never walked again without assistance. But he didn't let that stop him from pursuing his potential. Eight years later, he became the governor of New York, and in 1932, he was elected president of the United States.

Who else can you think of who has overcome tragedies or past mistakes to pursue his potential? You may even personally know some people who fought back from adversity to become successful.

_____

_____

_____

Let these people inspire you. No matter what you've faced in the past, you have the *potential* to overcome it.

4. FOCUS ON THE FUTURE

Baseball Hall of Famer Yogi Berra declared, "The future isn't what it used to be." Although that may be true, it's still the only place we have to go. Your potential lies ahead of you—whether you're eight, eighteen, forty-eight, or eighty. You still have room to improve yourself. You can become better tomorrow than you are today. As the Spanish proverb says, "He who does not look ahead remains behind."

List three exciting things that you have to look forward to in the coming months.

_____

_____

_____

When you know your purpose in life and are growing to reach your maximum potential, you're well on your way to being a success. But there is one more essential part of the success journey: helping others. Without that aspect, the journey can be a lonely and shallow experience.

SOWING SEEDS THAT BENEFIT OTHERS

It's been said that we make a living by what we get, but we make a life by what we give. Physician, theologian, and philosopher Albert Schweitzer stated it even more strongly: "The purpose of human life is to serve, and to show compassion and the will to help others." For him, the success journey led to Africa, where he served people for many years.

For you, sowing seeds that benefit others probably won't mean traveling to another country to serve the poor—unless that is the purpose you were born to fulfill. (And if it is, you won't be satisfied until that's what you're doing.) However, if you're like most people, helping others is something you can do right here at home, whether it's spending more time with your family, developing an employee who shows potential, helping people in the community, or putting your desires on hold for the sake of your team at work. The key is to find your purpose and help others while you're pursuing it. Entertainer Danny Thomas insisted, "All of us are born for a reason, but all of us don't discover why. Success in life has nothing to do with what you gain in life or accomplish for yourself. It's what you do for others."

What are you doing to invest in others?

_____

_____

_____

TAKE ACTION

Look back at the section of questions you answered concerning whom you should talk to, what you should read and watch, and what you should participate in. Pick an item from that list and plan to spend thirty minutes each day following through on it. Also spend time planning for next month—allotting time to shop for resources, set up meetings with people you can learn from, and for reading that will help you grow personally or professionally.

DAY 5

TAKE THE JOURNEY

As we finish up this week, think back to Day 1, when you read the story about my team moving from San Diego to Atlanta. At that time it was a surprise to me that so many people said yes to the move, and it got me thinking. Why were so many of them willing to be uprooted, leaving behind everything that was familiar, including family and friends, to move all the way across the country?

Why do you think the group was willing to take the trip?

_____

_____

_____

REASONS FOR TAKING THE TRIP

WE GAVE THEM A PICTURE OF WHERE THEY WERE GOING

As Dick, the two real-estate agents, and I spoke to our people, we gave them a picture of our future in Atlanta: the positive working environment, the greater number of lives that we would be able to touch, the improvement in their quality of life, and the opportunity that we as a company would have to go to the next level. They could see it all—the benefits to them personally and to the company.

WE ANSWERED THEIR QUESTIONS

The prospect of taking a journey can create insecurity and lead to numerous questions. Our people wanted to know where we would be locating the office, what Atlanta's schools were like, the condition of the housing market, the cultural and entertainment attractions available in the city, the state tax structure, and so on. In that first meeting, we were able to answer nearly all of their questions.

THEY HAD EXPERIENCED PERSONAL SUCCESS IN THEIR LIVES

As a team, INJOY was experiencing success, and so were the individuals. They were responsible for the company's success and at the same time were enjoying the fruits of that success. They had a sense of purpose. They were growing personally. And they were helping others.

THEY WERE NO LONGER THE SAME AND WANTED TO CONTINUE TO HAVE SIGNIFICANCE

A couple of weeks before we announced the move, I heard Patty Knoll, one of our employees, say, "I love working for INJOY, helping so many people through what we do. I can't imagine working anywhere else." Once a person has tasted success and realizes that her efforts have significance, it's something that she never forgets—and that she never wants to give up. Making a difference in the lives of others changes her outlook on life and her priorities.

> *Do you find that you are more often the person asking people to take the journey or the person being asked? Give an example.*

_____

_____

_____

As a leader, I tend to be the person asking others to come along with me on the journey. However, I also find myself using my gifts and talents to come alongside others so they can continue on their own success journey. But no matter which aspect of the journey you find yourself in, always strive to fulfill your purpose in life, keep growing to reach your potential, and sow seeds to benefit others. Don't just follow someone else's path. Create your own.

CHARTING THE COURSE

The journey you are setting out on has the potential of taking you a long way—maybe farther than you've dreamed. To take it, you'll need a picture of where you're going, answers to your questions about success, knowledge of what success is like, and the ability to change and keep growing. In the next few weeks we will review all of these topics in more depth, as we continue to chart out your Road Map for Success.

Week

2

WHERE WOULD I LIKE TO GO?

DAY 1
Your Dream Trip

DAY 2
The Power

DAY 3
The Start

DAY 4
The Pursuit

DAY 5
Commitment

PRINCIPAL QUESTIONS

DAY 1: Who do I dream about becoming?

DAY 2: What does my dream do for me?

DAY 3: What is my dream?

DAY 4: Whom should I share my dream with?

DAY 5: Am I committed or confused?

DAY 1

YOUR DREAM TRIP

My wife, Margaret, and I love to travel. I often ask other people where they would go if they could take a trip to anywhere in the world. I have gotten a variety of answers to that question, from Germany to Australia to Africa. I enjoyed talking with these folks about their dreams for travel. Their eyes lit up and their speech quickened as they pictured in their minds the places they would see and the activities in which they would participate.

If you could go anywhere in the world, where would you go?

_____

But I also asked them another question: Why haven't you taken your dream trip? Some people said they didn't want to go alone and were waiting until they found a traveling companion. Many said they didn't have the money. And others noted that they lacked the time.

What is holding you back from taking your dream trip?

_____

It's been my experience that we make time and set aside money for those things that are most important to us. All of the people who go on their dream trips don't have unlimited money and time. They make the journey because they plan ahead and they're willing to pay whatever price is required for them to go.

Now let me ask you another question: If you could go anywhere, where would you like to go? Not in terms of vacations, but in your life.

_____

_____

Your answer to that question does a lot to determine whether or not you're successful. You see, we're all on a journey, whether we know it or not. We are traveling inevitably toward the ends of our lives. So the real question for us is whether we're going to select a destination and steer a course for it, or allow ourselves to be swept along with the tide, letting others determine where we'll end up. The choice is entirely up to us.

A CRUISE TO NOWHERE

If you live in a town near the ocean, you may have seen advertisements for "cruises to nowhere." Maybe you've even been on one. People board a cruise ship, and when they leave the pier, instead of setting out for a lush island or other exotic location, they go out to sea and travel in circles for a couple of days. Meanwhile, they dine on sumptuous meals, lounge around the pool, enjoy the shows, and participate in onboard activities. It's similar to checking into a fine hotel or resort.

The problem for a lot of people is that their lives are too much like those cruises. They're on a trip with no set destination, no charted course. They're in a holding pattern, and they occupy their time pursuing pleasures or engaging in activities that don't have any lasting benefit for themselves or others. Meanwhile, they travel in circles. In the end, they finish no better than they started. A cruise to nowhere may be a fun way to occupy a few days of vacation time, but it's no way to spend your life.

As I mentioned before, success is a journey. You don't suddenly become successful when you arrive at a particular place or achieve a certain goal. But that doesn't mean you should travel without identifying a destination. You can't fulfill your purpose and grow toward your potential if you don't know what direction you should be going. You need to identify and sail toward your destination. In other words, you need to discover your dream.

TAKE ACTION

Set aside a block of time to think about and answer the following life questions.

What is my greatest passion—the thing I love doing so much that I would gladly do it for free?

_____

_____

_____

What is so important to me that I would be willing to die for it?

_____

_____

_____

Include reasons for your anwers.

DAY 2

THE POWER

I believe that each of us has a dream placed in the heart. I'm not talking about wanting to win the lottery. That kind of idea comes from a desire to escape our present circumstances, not to pursue a heartfelt dream. I'm talking about a vision deep inside that speaks to the very soul. It's the thing we were born to do. It draws on our talents and gifts. It appeals to our highest ideals. It sparks our feelings of destiny. It is inseparably linked to our purpose in life. The dream starts us on the success journey.

When I look for the name of a person who identified and lived out his dream, I think of auto industry pioneer and visionary Henry Ford. He asserted, "The whole secret of a successful life is to find out what it is one's destiny to do, and then do it."

Who is your favorite dreamer? What visionary action has he or she been able to accomplish?

_____

_____

_____

THE FIVE POWERS OF A DREAM

1. A DREAM GIVES US DIRECTION

Have you ever known a person who didn't have a clue concerning what she wanted in life, yet was highly successful? I haven't either. We all need something worthwhile for which to aim. A dream provides us with that. It acts as a compass, telling us the direction we should travel. And until we've identified that right direction, we'll never know for sure that our movement is actually progress. Our actions are just as likely to take us backward instead of forward. If you move in *any* direction other than toward your dream, you'll miss out on the opportunities necessary to be successful.

How are you currently moving in the direction of your dream?

_____

_____

_____

2. A DREAM INCREASES OUR POTENTIAL

Without a dream, we may struggle to see potential in ourselves because we don't look beyond our current circumstances. But with a dream, we begin to see ourselves in a new light, as having greater potential and being capable of stretching and growing to reach it. Every opportunity we meet, every resource we discover, every talent we develop, becomes a part of our potential to grow toward that dream. The greater the dream, the greater the potential. E. Paul Hovey said, "A blind man's world is bounded by the limits of his touch; an ignorant man's world by the limits of his knowledge; a great man's world by the limits of his vision." If your vision—your dream—is great, then so is your potential for success.

Do you consider your dream to be great? If so, why? If not, how can you modify your dream in order to aim higher?

_____

_____

_____

3. A DREAM HELPS US PRIORITIZE

A dream gives us hope for the future, and it also brings us power in the present. It makes it possible for us to prioritize everything we do. A person who has a dream knows what he is willing to *give up* in order to *go up*. He is able to measure everything he does according to whether or not it contributes to the dream, concentrating his attention on the things that bring him closer to it and giving less attention to everything that doesn't.

Ironically, many people do exactly the opposite. Rather than focus on one dream and let go of the less important things, some people want to keep every option open. But when they do, they actually face more problems because decision making becomes overly complicated for them.

When you keep your options open, at first it's fun to have so many possibilities before you. It seems to be an excellent idea. But as time goes by, you can't make any progress because you spend all your time preserving the options rather than moving forward.

When you have a dream, you don't have that problem. You can expend your time and energy on only those things that bring you closer to your dream. You let go of the distractions. They are unimportant. That knowledge frees up your time to concentrate on the few things that make a difference and it keeps you on the right track.

What distractions do you need to remove in order to focus more on your dream?

_____

_____

_____

4. A DREAM ADDS VALUE TO OUR WORK

A dream puts everything we do into perspective. Even the tasks that aren't exciting or immediately rewarding take on added value when we know they ultimately contribute to the fulfillment of a dream. Each activity becomes an important piece in that bigger picture. It reminds me of the story of a reporter who talked to three construction workers pouring concrete at a building site. "What are you doing?" he asked the first worker.

"I'm earning a paycheck," he grumbled.

The reporter asked the same question of a second laborer, who looked over his shoulder and said, "What's it look like I'm doing? I'm pouring concrete."

Then he noticed a third man who was smiling and whistling as he worked. "What are you doing?" he asked.

The worker stopped what he was doing and said excitedly, "I'm building a shelter for the homeless." He wiped his hands clean on a rag and then pointed, saying, "Look, over there is where the kitchen will be. And that over there is the women's dormitory. This here . . ."

Each man was doing the same job. But only the third was motivated by a larger vision. The work he did was fulfilling a dream, and it added value to all his efforts.

5. A DREAM PREDICTS OUR FUTURE

When we have a dream, we're not just spectators sitting back, hoping that everything turns out all right. We're taking an active part in shaping the meaning of our lives. And the winds of change don't simply blow us here and there. Our personal dreams, when pursued, are the most likely predictors of our future. That doesn't mean we have any guarantees, but it does increase our chances for success tremendously.

Dare to dream and to act on that dream. Dream in spite of problems, circumstances, and obstacles. History is filled with men and women who faced adversity and achieved success in spite of it. For example, the Greek orator Demosthenes stuttered! The first time he tried to make a public speech, he was laughed off the rostrum. But he had a dream of being a notable speaker. He pursued that dream and grew toward his potential. It is said that he used to put pebbles in his mouth and practice speaking over the sound of the crashing surf at the seashore. His persistence paid off. He lived his dream: he became the greatest orator of the ancient world.

Oliver Wendell Holmes noted, "The great thing in this world is not so much where we are but in what direction we are moving." This is also one of the great things about having a dream. You can pursue your dream no matter where you are today. And what happened in the past isn't as important as what lies ahead in the future. As the saying goes, "No matter what a person's past may have been, his future is spotless." You can begin pursuing your dream today!

TAKE ACTION

Meet with someone you believe to be living out his dream. This person doesn't need to be famous or rich, just someone who is obviously excited about and dedicated to the path he is on. Set up a time to talk about the five powers of a dream that you learned about today, and ask questions about this person's own success journey. Jot down notes from your conversation, and write the most beneficial piece of wisdom he gives you on a note card. Keep this note card in a place where you will see it often. It will be a reminder and encouragement as you pursue your own dream.

DAY 3

THE START

Over the years I've learned a lot about vision and what it means to have a dream because it's such a critical part of leadership. I've observed that there is a big difference between those who dream and those who make their dreams come true. As Nolan Bushnell, founder of Atari, said, "Everyone gets an idea in the shower. But the successful ones get out of the shower, dry off, and do something about it." Here are the first three stages in developing a successful dream, based on my personal experience and observation.

1. I THOUGHT IT

The whole process begins with the seed of an idea—a vision that grows out of a heartfelt desire. Many people discover their dream in a flash of insight after working in an area for years. Some receive it in a time of prayer. Others are motivated by events from their pasts. Maybe you've already experienced the "I Thought It" stage and discovered your dream. If you haven't, read the following steps that will help you clear away the clutter and discover (or fine-tune) your dream:

BELIEVE IN YOUR ABILITY TO SUCCEED

As I said before, no person can consistently perform in a manner that is inconsistent with the way he sees himself. You must believe that you *can* succeed if you *are* to succeed. You must acknowledge to yourself that you're capable of discovering your dream in order to find it. You don't have to be a genius, lucky, or rich. You just need to believe it can happen.

List a few reasons why you will be able to succeed.

_____

_____

_____

GET RID OF YOUR PRIDE

People full of themselves usually don't have much room left over for a life-changing dream. That's why it's so important to get rid of pride: it can keep you from trying new things or asking questions because you are afraid of looking stupid. It makes you want to stay in your comfort zone instead of striving for the end zone. Pride puts your focus on appearance instead of potential. And it prevents you from taking risks—something you must do to discover your dream.

What role does pride play in your life? How can you correct any negative effects it may have on your pursuit of your dream?

_____

_____

_____

CULTIVATE CONSTRUCTIVE DISCONTENT

Discontent is the driving force that makes people search for their dreams. Think about it: every invention registered in the United States Patent Office is the result of creative discontent. Each inventor, not satisfied with something as it was, found a way to constructively overcome his or her dissatisfaction, either by creating something new or by improving what already existed.

The same is true for you. Complacency never brings success. You must desire positive change. Only constructive discontent will motivate you to find your purpose and to grow to reach your potential. Earle Wilson commented, "If what you did yesterday still looks pretty big to you, then you haven't done enough today."

How does constructive discontent play a role in your dream?

_____

_____

_____

ESCAPE FROM HABIT

A habit can be defined as something you do without thinking. (Maybe that's why we have so many of them.) Habit can kill a dream because when you stop thinking, you stop questioning and dreaming. You begin to accept what *is* without considering what *could be*. Habit can cause you to go through the motions rather than think about the possibilities. It slowly closes the door on potential.

Examine all the things you're currently doing by rote. Then shake things up. Look to your horizons. What must you stop doing in order to pursue what you really care about?

_____

_____

_____

What are you currently doing that doesn't propel you in the direction of your purpose, develop your potential, or help other people? Can it be eliminated?

_____

_____

_____

BALANCE CREATIVITY WITH CHARACTER

Releasing your creativity to get yourself out of a rut and thinking about your dream is a basic part of the process, but nothing will come of it if you don't have the character to follow through with action. When it comes to a dream, a truly successful person has enough creativity to *think it out* and enough character to *try it out*. She has enough creativity to *picture it in her mind* and enough character to *produce it with her hands.* All the dreaming in the world won't do a bit of good unless you're ready to wake up and go to work.

> *In which area are you stronger: creativity or character? How does this affect the balance between creativity and character?*

_____

_____

_____

2. I CAUGHT IT

The moment you discover your dream—the thing you were created to do—is an incredible experience. But that alone is not enough to take you on the success journey. The development of a successful dream is a process. And the next step of development requires you to invest in your dream emotionally. It needs to grow beyond your thoughts and carry over into your feelings.

In 1935, Hubert H. Humphrey wrote a letter to his wife during his first trip to Washington, D.C. It captures the emotions of the then-twenty-four-year-old pharmacist from Minnesota. It says, "I can see how someday, if you and I just apply ourselves and make up our minds to work for bigger things, we can someday live here in Washington and probably be in government, politics or service . . . Oh gosh, I hope my dream comes true—I'm going to try anyhow." Humphrey's dream did come true. In 1946, he became the mayor of Minneapolis; in 1949, he successfully ran for the U.S. Senate; and in 1964, he served as the vice president of the United States under Lyndon B. Johnson. In all, Humphrey served in government for thirty-two years.

> *What do you feel when you share your dream with others, or when you take a step in the direction of your dream? (If you've never shared your dream with others, take a risk and do so.)*

_____

_____

_____

3. I SOUGHT IT

An old Italian proverb says, "Between saying and doing, many a pair of shoes is worn out." Lots of people have dreams. And many of them have strong feelings about them. But what separates the developer of a successful dream from a mere daydreamer is committed action. Between the "I Caught It" and "I Sought It" stages, dreams don't die—they fade away. It takes hunger, tenacity, and commitment to see a dream through until it becomes reality. Once you discover your dream, go after it.

What concrete actions have you recently taken in pursuit of your dream?

_____

_____

_____

TAKE ACTION

RECALL THE STAGES OF YOUR DREAM . . .

At what time did the "I Thought It" stage come into your life? How far back does your dream go? How did you first react to the idea? Briefly describe the "I Thought It" moment.

_____

_____

_____

What words describe the emotion of your dream?

_____

_____

_____

DAY 4

THE PURSUIT

You have thought it, caught it, and sought it, but now it's time to sustain it as you continue to pursue your dream. And the immediate danger, which follows the first three stages of your dream, is that the dream will be suddenly and deliberately shot down.

A FEW SHOT IT

During its early stages, a dream is an incredibly fragile thing. As corporate leadership expert Bobb Biehl says, "Dreams are like soap bubbles floating close to jagged rocks on a windy day."

Dreams are so fragile at this stage of the journey because they are so new. We haven't had time yet to let them grow or develop. They're not established, and they don't have a track record. When a seedling oak is only a year old, a child can tear it out by the roots. But once it's had some time to become firmly established, even the force of a hurricane may not knock it down.

Dreams are also more easily shot down at this point because close friends or family members are the usual attackers—they're the only ones who know about them. Our hopes and desires may be able to weather the criticism of a stranger, but they have a more difficult time surviving when undermined by a loved one.

> *When you share your dreams with friends and family, do they tend to support your aspirations or tear them down? Or are you keeping your dream to yourself because you anticipate a negative reaction from those close to you?*

_____

_____

In her book *Silver Boxes,* my friend Florence Littauer tells a story revealing the power over our dreams held by those who are close to us. It's about her mother-in-law, Marita Littauer. After knowing her for many years and being a little intimidated by her, Florence one day asked the aging woman what she would have been if she could have been anything she wanted. "An opera singer," Marita answered without hesitation. "I wanted to study music, but my parents felt that was a waste of time, that I'd make more money in the millinery business. But I was in one show in college, and I had the lead."

The memory of that dream never left Marita Littauer, even though her mother had shot it down. In her last days, her mind faded and she could no longer speak. But some evenings she would stand proudly by her chair and sing opera to her nurse. Even in the twilight of her years, that deep desire never left her. Florence said, "Mother had talent that was never developed, a music box that was never allowed to play, a career that was never begun. Mother died with the music still in her."[1]

What dream of yours has been shot down? Does that dream still linger in the back of your mind? Have you ever done anything to pursue that dream, or have you given it up?

_____

_____

_____

I GOT IT

Most people have no idea how close they are to breaking through and living their dream, to reaching the "I Got It" stage. Success is achieved in inches, not miles. For example, the average baseball player in major league baseball hits about .250. Another way to say it is that he gets a hit once for every four times he bats. Someone with average fielding skills who bats .250 can play in the major leagues, but he probably won't be remembered after he has left the game.

Contrast that with someone like Tony Gwynn, who spent his entire career with the San Diego Padres. He is considered one of the best hitters in baseball. He won eight National League batting championships in the twenty seasons he played. And on August 6, 2000, he became the twenty-second player in history to collect three thousand hits. Someday he'll be elected to the Baseball Hall of Fame in Cooperstown, New York.

If you didn't know baseball, you might expect that in order to be as successful as he is, Tony would be twice as good at hitting the ball as the average player. But that's not the case. As I write this, Tony has a lifetime batting average of .339. That means he gets a hit one in every three times at bat. You would have to go to several games to see the one extra hit Tony got compared to the average player hitting .250.

Your ability to live your dream may be closer than you think. You need dedication and perseverance, and you have to survive the doubts and criticisms of people closest to you, but you can make it to the "I Got It" stage.

How close do you think you are to living your dream?

❏ *I can hardly see the target, I'm so far away.*

❏ *I've come a ways, but I still have a ways to go.*

❏ *I'm so close that I'm almost there.*

SOME OTHERS FOUGHT IT

Unfortunately, not everyone will want to celebrate with you when your dream begins to become a reality. I think you'll find that people will fall into two groups:

- *Firefighters:* These people want to put out the fire that you have for your dream. No matter what you're for—they're against it. The way these kinds of people criticize everything, you'd think they get paid for it. And nothing you do or say can change their attitude.

- *Firelighters:* These people want to help you and are willing to do what they can to stoke the flames of your success even higher.

List a few of the firefighters and firelighters in your life:

Firefighters   Firelighters

_____   _____

_____   _____

_____   _____

_____   _____

When you're trying to realize your dream, sometimes you'll be surprised by which people want to light your fire and which ones want to put it out. Some people you consider friends will fight your success. Others will support you in ways you didn't expect. But no matter which people criticize you or how they do it, don't let them take your focus off your dream.

I TAUGHT IT

Any dream worth living is worth sharing with others. After all, that's a big part of what it means to be successful. But that's not how everyone looks at it. I've observed that when people realize their dream, they react in one of two ways. Some hold the dream close, trying to keep all of it for themselves. When they do, their dream often shrinks. Because they haven't shared it, they have to sustain it all by themselves. Everything depends on them. They don't get the help of others, the benefits of teamwork, or the joy of sharing their blessings.

But the person who shares her dream gets to watch it grow. The synergy of shared ideas often takes a dream to a whole new level. The dream becomes greater than the person launching it ever imagined it could be. And the others who participate in it often adopt it as their own dream.

As you give others an opportunity to share your dream, paint a broad picture for them so that they can catch your vision. You may want to include the following:

- *A Horizon:* to help them see the incredible possibilities ahead
- *The Sun:* to give them warmth and hope
- *Mountains:* to represent the challenges ahead
- *Birds:* to inspire them to soar like eagles
- *Flowers:* to remind them to stop and smell the roses, to enjoy the journey along the way
- *A Path:* to offer direction and security, to give assurance that you will be leading them the right way
- *Yourself:* to demonstrate your commitment to the dream to them
- *Them:* to show where they fit in and to communicate your belief in them

When you are willing to share the dream by including others, there is almost no limit to what you can accomplish. The impossible comes within reach.

OTHERS BOUGHT IT

If you live your dream and successfully share it, others will buy into it. People have a desire to follow a leader with a great dream. Now more than ever, people are looking for heroes. Unfortunately, many are looking in places that are likely to leave them disappointed: sports, music, movies, and television. But real heroes are leaders who can help others achieve success, people who take others with them. And it all begins with a dream. As Winifred Newman said, "Vision is the world's most desperate need. There are no hopeless situations, only people who think hopelessly."

TAKE ACTION

Prepare yourself to share your dream with others.

Write out your dream according to the analogy in this chapter:

Horizon: _____

Sun: _____

Mountains: _____

Birds: _____

Flowers: _____

Path: _____

Yourself: _____

Them: (This will depend on the individual person.) _____
_____

DAY 5

COMMITMENT

If you haven't already discovered your dream, you're probably realizing how much you've been missing. A dream will provide you with a reason to get up every day, a path to follow, and a target to hit. Besides, as Yogi Berra remarked, "If you don't know where you are going, you might wind up someplace else." Wouldn't you say it's about time you got started?

A few years ago, I saw a segment on television's *Sixty Minutes* in which Mike Wallace was interviewing one of the Sherpa guides from Nepal who help climbers reach the top of Mount Everest.

"Why do you do it?" Wallace asked.

"To help others do something they cannot do on their own," answered the guide.

"But there are so many risks, so many dangers," said Wallace. "Why do you insist on taking people to the top of the mountain?"

The guide smiled and said, "It's obvious that *you've* never been to the top."

GO FOR THE DREAM

Going to the top takes a dream and a strong commitment. The greater the journey, the more committed you have to be to take it. As you prepare to continue on your success journey, make a commitment to yourself to find your dream and follow it. The road that lies before you is one that I know well because I made that commitment and have traveled on the journey for more than thirty years. I will travel alongside you until you are ready to carry on without me. But no matter how much help I can give, you won't make it without a commitment.

Take a look at the statement in the box below. Examine what it will mean to commit yourself to the journey, and sign it. Then be prepared to begin living your dream.

COMMITMENT TO THE SUCCESS JOURNEY

I commit myself to being successful. I recognize that success is a process, not a destination. I will discover my dream and do what I can to . . .

> Know my purpose in life,
> Grow to reach my maximum potential, and
> Sow seeds that benefit others.

Although the road may get bumpy, and it may require me to learn a new way of looking at life, I will do what it takes and persevere. I will take the success journey.

Signature: _____Date: _____

The potential for greatness lives within each of us. The key to achieving greatness is found when we discover and then develop our dream. You are on your way!

CHARTING THE COURSE

Turn to "My Road Map for Success" in the back of the workbook and complete Section A under *Knowing My Purpose.*

Week

3

How Far Can I Go?

PRINCIPAL QUESTIONS

DAY 1: Why is my attitude so important?

DAY 2: How has my attitude affected my opportunities?

DAY 3: What type of attitude do I display?

DAY 4: How can I improve my attitude?

DAY 5: Is my attitude helping or hurting my success journey?

DAY 1

ATTITUDE MATTERS

Whenever I travel to Washington, D.C., I try my best to get to the Smithsonian Institution. I love history, especially that of the United States, and the Smithsonian houses incredible artifacts and displays from our nation's two-hundred-plus years. Of all the exhibits, my favorite shows a video clip of a speech President John F. Kennedy made to Congress on May 25, 1961. Every time I see it I get goose bumps. It records the moment that Kennedy called America to execute the most astonishing and improbable real-life journey ever conceived. He cast the vision for the achievement of an idea that had been written about as early as A.D. 160 by Greek satirist Lucian of Samosata and thought about for eighteen hundred years since then. Kennedy said, "I believe that this nation should commit itself to achieving the goal before [the] decade is out, of landing a man on the moon and returning him safely to earth."

With today's popularity of science-fiction stories, traveling to the moon seems almost mundane. After all, on television you can see people living in deep space or trekking around the galaxy every day of the week. But in 1961, it was just about the wildest goal imaginable. Today it would be like proposing that a person swim the Pacific Ocean from California to Japan—and back again.

Back in the late 1950s and early 1960s, America was in a space race with the Soviet Union, and we were falling way behind. I was about ten years old when we heard that the USSR had launched the first satellite, *Sputnik*, into orbit. It felt like going to bed one night as the best athlete in your school and waking up the next morning only to find out that Babe Ruth was the new kid in class. What a shock! Then they launched *Sputnik II*, which carried the first space traveler, Laika the dog. And in 1959, they sent off *Luna I*, the first spacecraft to escape the earth's gravitational field and fly by the moon. The Soviets seemed to be landing one knockout punch after another. They also sent the first man into space, and one of their ships made the first orbit of the earth. The Soviets were winning.

In the midst of the hopelessness of the situation, President John F. Kennedy came forward, stood before the United States Congress, and said we would see a man on the moon by the end of the decade. Most people thought it was impossible. Even some of the people running NASA thought it couldn't be done. They were the ones who told Kennedy they wanted to do it someday, but it had been only a *dream*. The technology required to make it happen didn't exist, and they weren't sure that it could exist. But that didn't stop Kennedy. He not only made the impossible our goal, but he gave it a deadline.

Despite all the doubts, on July 16, 1969, *Apollo 11* lifted off from pad 39 at Kennedy Space Center and began a journey of 244,930 miles to the moon. Four days later, Neil Armstrong and Buzz Aldrin Jr. landed the lunar module *Eagle* on the surface of the moon. Five hundred million people watched on television as Armstrong took his first step into the powder-fine gray dust of the moon and uttered his famous line, "That's one small step for man, one giant leap for mankind." We had done it. We had achieved the impossible! What an awesome event in human history!

YOUR ATTITUDE DETERMINES YOUR ALTITUDE

That trip shouldn't have been possible, but it happened. Incredibly, the Soviets (and now the Russians), who were so far ahead of us in 1961, still have not put anyone on the moon.

What propelled the United States to accomplish such a feat—and in record time?

_____

_____

_____

I don't think it was the strength of our technology or the Cold War threat of Soviet superiority, although they were factors. I think we put people on the moon because we believed we could do it. In the blink of an eye, John F. Kennedy's speech took the idea of a lunar landing and changed it from an impossible dream to an obtainable target. It hardly mattered where we were technologically. A moon landing became a reality because of a change in *attitude*. You see, when our attitudes outdistance our abilities, even the impossible becomes possible.

I've talked to people who worked in the space program, and they have told me that the atmosphere was electric with expectation back then. Every day as they worked, one thought was foremost in their minds: *We're putting a man on the moon!* The president's goal contained the dream and prompted the positive attitude needed to make it happen.

That's the power of a dream coupled with the right attitude. If you have one without the other, you can't go very far on the journey.

- A dream without a positive attitude produces a daydreamer.

- A positive attitude without a dream produces a pleasant person who can't progress.

- A dream together with a positive attitude produces a person with unlimited possibilities and potential.

To go far, you need both a dream and a positive attitude. Kennedy knew that. A dream by itself won't do it. In fact, your attitude isn't just a necessary contributor for you to be successful. Your attitude—not intelligence, talent, education, technical ability, opportunity, or even hard work—is the main factor that determines whether you will live your dream. Attitude determines how far you can go on the success journey.

Yogi Berra, whose comments always seem to contain both humor and truth, said, "Life is like baseball; it's 95 percent mental and the other half is physical." Despite the unusual math, Berra knew how much the average person underestimates the role of the mind in the success process. If you have intelligence, talent, education, technical know-how, opportunities, and a strong work ethic, yet lack the right attitude, you will never enjoy the success journey. That may be a revolutionary idea to you, so I'm going to say that again: If you don't have a good attitude, you will never enjoy the success journey. Having a good attitude makes all the difference in the world. Lowell Peacock remarked, "Attitude is the first quality that marks the successful man. If he has a positive attitude and is a positive thinker, who likes challenges and difficult situations, then he has half his success achieved."

TAKE ACTION

Think about a famous person whom you admire. It can be someone from history, business, sports, or another area of interest. Now look at a few quotes from this person. (An easy way to do this is on the Internet if you have access.) How is their attitude reflected in their words? How do you think their attitude has factored into their accomplishments? How are your own words a reflection of your attitude?

Your Future Is Determined by the Sum
of Your Attitude

Psychologist-philosopher William James said, "The greatest discovery of my generation is that people can alter their lives by altering their attitudes of mind." The choices you've made up to now have come as the result of your attitude. Your attitude determines your actions, and your actions determine your accomplishment. You may or may not like to think about it, but the person you are and where you are today are the result of your attitude.

When you're born, everything is out of your control. You don't choose who your biological parents are, when and where you're born, or any of your circumstances. But as you grow older, you start making decisions, and you become accountable for what happens in your life. In adolescence, the number of decisions you make multiplies, and by the time you reach the end of your second decade, your choices are all your own, whether you like to admit it or not. Right now, if you're over twenty-one, you're completely responsible for your choices—and your attitude.

Write about a decision you made last year and how your attitude at that time influenced your decision and following actions.

_____

_____

_____

YOUR CURRENT ATTITUDE IS A CHOICE

Most people with bad attitudes usually point to something other than themselves to explain their problem. But you can't rightfully blame your attitude on anything or anyone but yourself. It's not what happens *to* you but what happens *in* you that counts. Your attitude is not based on . . .

- *Circumstances:* You may not be able to control what happens to you, but you are completely responsible for your reaction to what happens to you.

- *Upbringing:* The past is gone and outside your control. You are responsible for not allowing it to control you in the present.

- *Limitations:* Since everyone faces limitations of some kind—whether lack of talent, limited money, few opportunities, or poor appearance—you need to learn to live with them. As Robert Schuller said, "Your limitations should be guidelines, not stop signs. They should direct and guide your path on the journey, not prevent you from taking it."

- *Others:* No one but you is responsible for the choices you make. You have been hurt or abused in the past, but it's up to you to overcome that injury—just as you would a physical one—and move beyond it.

The truth is that anyone, no matter how good the circumstances are, can find a reason to have a negative attitude. And everyone, no matter how bad the circumstances are, can find a way to maintain a good attitude.

What circumstances could you point to as reasons to justify a bad attitude?

_____

_____

_____

What have you done to overcome and move past those circumstances, which might otherwise negatively affect your attitude?

_____

_____

_____

One of the greatest discoveries you can ever make is that you can change. No matter where you were yesterday or how negative your attitudes have been in the past, you can be more positive today. And that makes an incredible difference in your potential and life.

A quote over a door in the Phoenix Suns' locker room sums up the importance of choosing a positive attitude. It came from former Boston Celtic Bill Russell. It says: "The game is scheduled, we have to play it—we might as well win." What a wonderful insight—and from a real winner. While Russell played with the Celtics, they won an incredible eleven NBA titles in thirteen years. Having a positive attitude worked for him, and it can work for you.

How does Bill Russell's quote relate to your own life and attitude?

_____

_____

_____

YOUR ATTITUDE DETERMINES HOW YOU APPROACH THE JOURNEY

Several years ago, an experiment was performed in a school in the San Francisco Bay area. A principal called in three teachers and said, "Because you are the finest teachers in the system and you have the greatest expertise, we're going to give you ninety selected high-IQ students. We're going to let you move these students through this next year at their pace and see how much they can learn."

The three faculty members, the students, and the students' parents thought it was a great idea. And they all especially enjoyed the school year. By the time school ended, the students had achieved from 20 to 30 percent more than the other students in the entire San Francisco Bay area had.

At the end of the year, the principal called in the three teachers and told them, "I have a confession to make. You did not have ninety of the most intellectually prominent students. They were run-of-the-mill students. We took ninety students at random from the system and gave them to you."

The teachers naturally concluded that their exceptional teaching skills must have been responsible for the students' great progress.

"I have another confession," said the principal. "You're not the brightest of the teachers. Your names were the first three drawn out of a hat."

Why, then, did the students and teachers perform at such an exceptional level for an entire year? The answer can be found in their attitudes. They had an attitude of positive expectation—the teachers and students believed in themselves and one another. They performed well because they believed they could.[1]

Your attitude toward life determines life's attitude toward you. How you think affects your approach to the success journey in a powerful way.

> What I believe about life determines
> How I perceive life, which determines
> What I receive from life.

If you expect the worst, you will certainly get it. If you expect the best, even when negative circumstances come your way—and they will because a positive attitude doesn't stop them—you can make the best of it and keep going.

Are you more of a glass-is-half-empty or a glass-is-half-full type of person?

❏ *Half-Full*

❏ *Half-Empty*

Describe how you approached your most recent major assignment or task at home or work.

_____

_____

_____

TAKE ACTION

Present the following scenario (or a similar one) to two different people. The first person you approach should be someone you know to have a positive attitude. The second person should be someone who you know has a negative attitude.

SCENARIO: A special event (like your anniversary or best friend's birthday) is taking place on Saturday, but your boss wants you to work Saturday on a big project that has the possibility of advancing your career. What should you do?

Examine the differences in their answers. How did their suggestions reflect their positive or negative attitude?

DAY 3

ACCENTUATE THE POSITIVE

If you talk to people in the top organizations across the country, the higher you go, the better the attitudes you'll discover. A Fortune 500 study found that 94 percent of all the executives surveyed attributed their success more to attitude than any other factor.[2] That just goes to show you that if you want to go far, have a good attitude.

Attitude affects more than just your ability to succeed in business. It affects every aspect of your life—even your health. I once read an article about a study at King's College Hospital in London. It was conducted among cancer patients who had undergone mastectomies. Researchers at the hospital tracked the progress of fifty-seven women. Of the ones who had a positive attitude when they were diagnosed with cancer, seven out of ten were still living ten years later. But of the ones who felt a sense of hopelessness during diagnosis, eight of ten had died.[3] Ongoing medical research continues to present similar findings. You can go a lot farther in life—and live longer—with a good attitude than you can without one.

How has your attitude made a situation either better or worse in the last few days?

_____

_____

_____

YOUR ATTITUDE MEANS THE DIFFERENCE BETWEEN SUCCESS AND FAILURE

A good attitude makes it possible for you to be successful. It gives you fuel so that you want to pursue your purpose, grow to your potential, and sow seeds benefiting others. It can give you the staying power to improve. But it also makes the journey more enjoyable along the way—no matter where it takes you. As former UCLA basketball coach John Wooden said, "Things turn out the best for the people who make the best of the way things turn out."

Think about the last time you traveled. Chances are, there were some unexpected delays or bumps in your journey. How did you handle the unexpected? What effect did your attitude have on your trip?

_____

_____

_____

You can change your attitude. You may not be able to change other things about yourself, but you can definitely make your attitude more positive. If you try, you'll soon discover that the best helping hand is at the end of your own arm.

SEVEN SIGNS OF A GREAT ATTITUDE

What does it mean to have a great attitude? I believe positive people share seven qualities.

1. BELIEF IN SELF

Herb True observed, "Many people succeed when others do not believe in them. But rarely does a person succeed when he does not believe in himself." He was exactly right. Positive self-worth is a prime characteristic of a person with a good attitude.

Anyone who doesn't believe in herself expects the worst not only of herself but also of others. If you have low self-confidence, you will likely have to struggle to focus on anything but yourself because you will always be worried about how you look, what others think about you, and whether you're going to fail. But when you believe in yourself, you're free to see yourself in a more objective light and focus on improving yourself and reaching your potential. And that makes all the difference. No wonder psychologist Dr. Joyce Brothers said, "It is no exaggeration to say that a strong, positive self-image is the best possible preparation for success in life."

Do you believe in yourself, or do you find yourself overly concerned about your appearance and what you might do or say when you are around others? (Check one)

- ❑ *I am confident in my potential and abilities. I find it easy to talk to people and face new challenges.*

- ❑ *Sometimes I feel a little unsure about myself around others, but it doesn't negatively affect my daily actions.*

- ❑ *I just know people are looking at me and judging me. I prefer staying out of people's way.*

If you checked the last box, you need to work on your self-confidence. Enlist the help of a friend, and together name some of your strengths and discover the things you have to be positive about.

2. WILLINGNESS TO SEE THE BEST IN OTHERS

I've never known a positive person yet who didn't love people and try to see the good in them. An effective way to help you see the best in others is to do what I call putting a "10" on people's heads. Here's what I mean: We all have expectations of others. But we can choose whether the expectations are negative or positive. We can think that others are totally worthless or absolutely wonderful. When we make the decision to expect the best, and we look for the good instead of the bad, we're seeing them as a "10."

The ability to do this with others is significant for a couple of reasons. First, you usually see in others what you expect to see. If you constantly expect and see good things in others, it's much easier to maintain a positive attitude. Second, people generally rise to meet your level of expectation. If you treat them positively, they tend to treat you the same way. If you expect them to get the job done and you show your confidence in them, they usually succeed. And on the relatively rare occasions when people don't treat you well, it's easy for you not to take their behavior personally because you know you have done your best, and you can move on without letting it affect your attitude.

What can you do to express confidence in your family, friends, and/or the people you work with?

_____

_____

_____

Pick people to "expect the best of" this week, and see if it influences their willingness to get the job done. Also take note of how they treat you in return.

3. ABILITY TO SEE OPPORTUNITY EVERYWHERE

Greek philosopher Plutarch wrote, "As bees extract honey from thyme, the strongest and driest of herbs, so sensible men often get advantage and profit from the most awkward circumstances." No matter what the circumstances, positive people see opportunities everywhere. They understand that opportunities aren't based on luck or position. They are the result of the right attitude. Opportunity exists where you find it.

What is the oddest or most unlikely place where you have found opportunity in the past?

_____

_____

_____

A statement in *Success* magazine made by Lois Wyse, president of Wyse Advertising, Inc., impressed me because it displayed an understanding of the importance of a positive attitude and how to apply it in everyday life. She said, "I tell my daughter, 'Always say yes, because nothing ever happens to people who say no.'" That can be very good business advice. It's obvious that she believes there are opportunities waiting to be seized.

Find one (nonharmful) thing to say yes to today, which you normally would have said no to in the past. Example: taking time out to go to lunch with people from work or helping someone with a problem for which you may not have all the answers. How could these two events provide opportunity?

_____

_____

_____

4. FOCUS ON SOLUTIONS

Likewise, people with a positive attitude focus their time and attention on solutions, not problems. Just about anybody can see problems. That doesn't take anything special. But positive people maintain a solution mind-set, seeing a solution in every problem and a possibility in every impossibility. As noted by Louis D. Brandeis, the Supreme Court justice after whom Brandeis University was named, "Most of the things worth doing in the world had been declared impossible before they were done."

Give an example of something you or someone else has accomplished that was said to be impossible.

----

5. Desire to Give

Nothing has as much positive impact on people as giving to others. People who have a giving spirit are some of the most positive people I know, because giving is the highest level of living. They focus their time and energy on what they can give to others rather than on what they can get from them. And the more people give, the better their attitude.

How often do you give to others? (Give an example of how you give.)

Has giving been a positive or negative experience for you?

Do you give more now, or have you reduced the amount compared to how you have given in the past?

Most unsuccessful people don't understand the concept of giving. They believe that how much people give and their attitude about it should be based on how much they have. But that's not true. I know many people who have very little but are tremendous givers. And I know people who have been blessed with money, good families, and wonderful careers who are stingy and suspicious of others. It's not what you have that makes a difference. It's what you do with what you have. And that is based completely on attitude.

What is your attitude when it comes to giving?

- ❑ *Whenever I see or hear about an opportunity to give, I jump right in.*

- ❑ *I give only when I know that my time or money will be spent well.*

- ❑ *I work so hard for what I have, I am reluctant to give to others.*

6. PERSISTENCE

Don B. Owens Jr. stated, "Many people fail in life because they believe in the adage: If you don't succeed, try something else. But success eludes those who follow such advice . . . The dreams that have come true did so because people stuck to their ambitions. They refused to be discouraged. They never let disappointment get the upper hand. Challenges only spurred them on to greater effort." Those characteristics—the ability to stick with it, overcome discouragement, and keep going in the face of disappointment—are all the results of a good attitude.

Describe a time when you "hung in there" and saw great results because of your persistence. What was your attitude like at the time?

_____

_____

_____

_____

When you have a positive attitude, it's easier to be persistent. If you think success is just around the corner, you keep going. When you believe everything turns out for the best, you don't mind a little discomfort. And when everything goes haywire, you remain persistent if you have a positive attitude; after all, you believe help is already on the way.

7. RESPONSIBILITY FOR THEIR LIVES

The final characteristic of positive people is their willingness to take responsibility for their own lives. Unsuccessful people duck responsibility. But a successful person understands that nothing positive happens until he's willing to step forward and take full responsibility for his thoughts and actions. Only when you're responsible for yourself can you look at yourself honestly, assess your strengths and weaknesses, and begin to change.

TAKE ACTION

Of the seven qualities of a positive attitude, which do you struggle with the most? Find a way to work on that area of your attitude for the next seven days. Have a person who knows you well and is around you frequently (your spouse, a coworker, or a friend) give you updates on how he thinks you are doing.

List the strategic actions you took to improve your attitude.

_____

_____

_____

_____

THE ATTITUDE ASSIGNMENT

W. W. Ziege said, "Nothing can stop the man with the right mental attitude from achieving his goal; nothing on earth can help the man with the wrong mental attitude." If I could share only one thing that I possess, it would be my way of thinking, for that more than anything else has helped me the most on the success journey. Attitude has always been my greatest asset, and it can be yours too. Andrew Carnegie asserted, "The man who acquires the ability to take full possession of his own mind may take possession of anything else to which he is justly entitled."

If you're constantly in a battle to keep your attitude positive, you can use some help. Here are some tips to assist you in taking full possession of your mind and making your thinking positively powerful.

EMPOWERED POSITIVE THINKING

CLAIM RESPONSIBILITIES, NOT RIGHTS

A predominant source of discontent among people derives from their fight to secure their rights. Think about your situation. Have you ever been wronged? Have there been times when you haven't gotten everything you deserved? Your answer to these questions is almost certainly yes. We live in an imperfect world, and because of that, as long as we live, we won't see a time when everything we do is rewarded justly.

So you're faced with a decision. Are you going to spend your time and energy on *what should have been*, or are you going to focus on *what can be*? Even when truth and justice are on your side, you may never be able to right your wrongs. Continually fighting for your rights in an imperfect world can make you resentful, angry, hateful, and bitter. These destructive emotions tap your energy and make you negative.

And besides, when you focus on your rights, you're often looking backward rather than forward. You can't make any progress when you're facing the wrong way. Glenn Clark remarked, "If you wish to travel far and fast, travel light. Take off all your envies, jealousies, unforgiveness, selfishness, and fears."

Which best describes your attitude?

- ❑ *That's life. Sometimes it's fair, and sometimes it's not.*
- ❑ *Life's not fair, and I deserve justice.*

When you stop worrying about your rights, you turn your focus in the right direction, and you can move forward on the journey. You recognize the wrongs, but you forgive them and focus on what you can control—your responsibilities. Doing that increases your energy, builds potential, and improves your prospects.

What wrongs do you need to let go of and forgive, in order to move forward on your success journey?

_____

ASSOCIATE WITH POSITIVE PEOPLE

Charles "Tremendous" Jones said that the only difference between who you are today and the person you will be in five years will come from the books you read and the people with whom you associate. The folks you spend your time with especially influence your attitude. The old adage is true: Birds of a feather do flock together.

Name the six people you spend the most time with.

_____   _____
_____   _____
_____   _____

Think about the people you listed, and others with whom you spend a good amount of time. Although you are born into a family, and you may not be able to choose the people you work with, you can choose your closest friends. If you choose negative friends, you are also choosing to have a negative attitude. But when you spend time with positive people, you help yourself to see things in a better light. Henry Ford maintained, "My best friend is the one who brings out the best in me." Think about what your friends bring out in you, and if it's not your best, it might be time for you to make some changes.

Look at the names you listed. Circle the names of the friends who are positive and help you to be a better person. Think of ways you can spend more time with these people.

MAKE THE PRESENT MOMENT YOUR HAPPIEST

U.S. diplomat and former child star Shirley Temple Black told a story about her husband, Charles, and his mother. When Charles was a boy, he asked his mother what the happiest moment of her life was.

"This moment—right now," she responded.

"But what about all the other happy moments in your life?" he said, surprised. "What about when you were married?"

"My happiest moment then was then," she answered. "My happiest moment now is now. You can only really live in the moment you're in. So to me, that's always the happiest moment."

Do you feel happiest when you are:

❑ *Planning for an event?*

❑ *Participating in an event?*

❑ *Reminiscing about an event?*

Charles Black's mother showed wisdom in her statement. Whenever you focus on the past or the future, you rob the present of its potential. But when you give your attention to what's happening at the moment and try to have a positive attitude about it, you open yourself up to all the possibilities that the present holds.

FIND WAYS TO RELIEVE STRESS

Stress fatigues people and pushes them toward negative thinking. That's why it's so important to find ways to release tension and regroup mentally. I love to play golf. It gives me both physical and mental releases. The scenery is beautiful, the game is challenging, and I enjoy the company of my fellow players.

There is another thing I like about playing golf. Whenever I've had a particularly tough time dealing with a difficult person, I relieve that stress on the golf course. I'll take a felt-tipped pen, write the name of whoever is bothering me on the ball, and tee it up for a long drive. Then I try to hit that ball as far as I can. I feel better, and even if I hit the ball off the fairway, it's no big deal. I may have lost a stroke and a ball, but I've also mentally gotten rid of my bothersome friend.

Find a positive way to release stress in your life. I recommend something active that requires both mental concentration and physical effort. Play golf, shoot darts, hit baseballs, play racquet ball, dig in your garden, or go for long walks with a friend. What you do is not important as long as it relieves stress and has a positive impact on your thinking and health.

What can you do to relieve stress?

_____

DON'T TAKE YOURSELF TOO SERIOUSLY

I heard a story about three business professionals who were comparing ideas on what it meant to be a success. "I'd say I had arrived," said the first, "if I were summoned to the White House for a private, personal meeting with the president of the United States."

"To me," said the second person, "success would mean meeting with the president in the Oval Office, having the hot line ring during our talk, and watching the president ignore it."

"No, you've both got it wrong," said the third one. "You're a success if you're privately consulting with the president, the hot line rings, he picks it up, and says, 'It's for you.'"

The problem with many unsuccessful people is that they take themselves too seriously. They think of success in the same way the three people in the story did. But success depends more on your attitude than it does on how important you think you are. Life should be fun. Even if your job is important and should be taken seriously, that doesn't mean you should take *yourself* seriously. You'll go farther in life and have a better time doing it if you maintain a sense of humor, especially when it comes to yourself.

TAKE ACTION TO CHANGE YOUR ATTITUDE

The quality of your life and the duration of your success journey depend on your attitude, and you are the only person in this world with the power to make it better. Dr. William Glasser maintained, "If you want to change attitudes, start with a change in behavior. In other words, begin to act the part, as well as you can, of the person you would rather be, the person you most want to become. Gradually, the old, fearful person will fade away."

Change requires action. Most people wait until they feel like it to change their attitudes. But that only causes them to keep waiting, because they have the whole process backward. If you wait until you *feel like it* to try to change your attitude, you will never change. You have to *act* yourself into changing.

An act of your will
Will lead you to action;
And your positive action
Will lead to a positive attitude!

TAKE ACTION

Choose one of the areas from today's lesson to work on. If you chose stress relief, go to the gym or hit the garden detail after work. If you chose surrounding yourself with positive people, set up a time during the day to call and talk or to meet with one of your most positive friends. The idea is to get started on shaping your attitude so you can increase your potential for success.

YOUR ATTITUDE CARRIES OVER

According to Henry Ford, "Whether you think you can or think you can't—you are right." The mind, more than anything else, determines how far you can go on the success journey. Let me show you what I mean by telling you a story about my friend Paul Nanney. He is about my age, and I've known him for more than fifteen years. His positive attitude has not only helped him to be a success, but it has actually saved his life.

Paul has several hobbies and interests. His favorite is flying, which he has been doing since he was a teenager. In 1976, Paul decided to take his interest to a new level. He planned a solo trip around the world in a Piper Cub airplane. Flying around the world seems like a difficult feat in itself. But it really takes on added significance when you realize that a Piper Cub is a very lightweight plane whose wings and fuselage are made of fabric. And before Paul tried it, no one had ever made an official flight around the world in an aircraft that light (less than one thousand kilos). As Paul later told others about his trip over the North Atlantic Ocean, "I felt that I had a lot in common with Lindbergh—except that he had a bigger and better-equipped plane."

Paul's journey started in San Diego and took him across the United States and into Canada. That was smooth flying, but the rest of the trip turned out to be a series of problems, trials, and near disasters. In Greenland, his plane's wings iced up, and he was forced to retrace part of his journey. He fought gale-force winds. In the Mediterranean, he discovered the generations-old animosity between the Greeks and the Turks when he stated his intention to fly from Kerkyra, Greece, to Istanbul, Turkey. A Greek official told him, "You cannot fly there from here. They will shoot down your plane. And if they don't, we certainly will."

He also encountered dozens of other problems, such as trying to find fuel in the Middle East, spending an entire day traveling to an oil refinery in Delhi to get two liters of oil, and flying through harrowing monsoons over the Bay of Bengal. Paul said that was the toughest flying he had ever done. For ten and a half horrific hours, as he flew through a series of thunderheads, his plane was blown around like a piece of paper, shooting up to as high as eighteen thousand feet one moment and suddenly dropping to as low as one thousand. As he fought with the controls of the aircraft, all he could think about was his fear of sharks and how they would be waiting for him in the ocean if he crashed.

As Paul proceeded on his trip, his positive attitude was his strongest ally. Not only did it bring him through the monsoons and repeated problems with customs agents and aviation officials, but it also kept his spirits up when he hit lengthy delays, such as when he sat in Manila for a week trying to get permission to fly to Japan. But Paul's attitude served him best during what turned out to be the last part of his journey.

After waiting out bad weather in Japan for a week, Paul finally took off for the Aleutian Islands off the coast of Alaska. It was to be the longest leg of his journey, and there would be little room for error because of the amount of fuel the flight would take. Even if everything went perfectly, in order to make it he would have to make an intentional emergency landing at an off-limits Strategic Air Command base when his fuel ran low.

But Paul had a problem during his flight. When he was about midway, he received an updated weather report that prompted him to change course. He was navigating without sophisticated electronic equipment, using only a compass and a watch, so he was planning on finding the island base and using its homing beacon once he was close enough to it. But he didn't know that the base's homing beacon wasn't transmitting. And on top of that, the late weather report he had received was faulty, so he was far off course. There was nothing but ocean as far as he could see—and he ran out of fuel.

The good attitude that had kept him positive during customs and logistics problems was put to a greater test. It would determine whether he would live or die.

A pilot from a nearby military aircraft talked to Paul as his plane glided down toward the ocean surface. He was solemn and asked Paul whether he had any last requests. Despite the odds, Paul was confident that he would make it, and he did. He crashed into the forty-degree water of the North Pacific Ocean, and he hung on there for two and a half hours until a Japanese fishing boat picked him up—something the doctors later told him was impossible because of the temperature. He lost his plane and his chance at the world record he was trying to set, but he lived to tell the story. "The whole thing was a 'Huck Finn' adventure from the very beginning," said Paul. "From the moment I took off, I wasn't sure exactly what would happen or where I would land. But I knew that I would make it."

Playwright Neil Simon urged, "Don't listen to those who say, 'It's not done that way.' Maybe it's not, but maybe you'll do it anyway. Don't listen to those who say, 'You're taking too big a chance.' Michelangelo would have painted the Sistine floor, and it would surely be rubbed out today."

That's the kind of spirit Paul had, and his positive attitude carried him through. "I learned long ago that I couldn't listen to everyone who told me I couldn't do something," said Paul. "If I had, I never would have even gotten started on that trip." Nor would he have made it almost around the world. His attitude has taken him a long way, both in the air and on the success journey.

Continue to ask yourself:

> *What is the condition of my attitude?*
> *Will it take me very far on the success journey?*

CHARTING THE COURSE

Turn to "My Road Map for Success" in the back of the workbook and complete Section B under *Knowing My Purpose.*

Week

4

HOW DO I GET THERE FROM HERE?

DAY 1
The Travelers

DAY 2
The Route

DAY 3
Finding Your Purpose

DAY 4
Defining Your Goals

DAY 5
And . . . Action!

PRINCIPAL QUESTIONS

DAY 1: Is my life just one long Sunday drive?

DAY 2: What are the benefits of having goals?

DAY 3: What is my purpose?

DAY 4: What are my goals?

DAY 5: What actions can I take to meet my goals?

DAY 1

THE TRAVELERS

When was the last time you went for a Sunday drive? That's not a very popular activity these days, but it sure was when I was growing up. And it was the favorite activity of the Raimeys, some wonderful neighbors I had as a kid. Mr. Raimey would say, "Come on, everybody. Let's pack up the car and go for a ride." Then he rounded up the family and occasionally a neighbor kid like me who was playing over at their house. And off we would go.

We lived in Circleville, Ohio, and our Sunday drives would take us to exotic places such as Lancaster, Chillicothe, or even Columbus. It seemed like a great adventure. Mr. Raimey would drive the dirt roads and highways that wound through the farms and fields of central Ohio. We never knew for sure what we might see.

Those Sunday drives were fun. And if we were lucky, as we would come across a little country store on the highway, Mr. Raimey would stop the car, and we would all pile out so that he and Mrs. Raimey could buy each of us a Coke or an ice cream. It was a wonderful way to spend an afternoon.

To tell you the truth, over the years I've met a lot of people who treat *life* a lot like a Sunday drive. They seem to be saying, "Let's just go and we'll see where we end up." They're willing to let life take them anywhere it wants to. I'm no scientist, but I've noticed that gravity tends to pull everything downward. And without some planning and direction, a person's life can do the same thing.

Which best describes your life:

- ❏ *I know where I'm going. In fact, my life is so well planned that I could tell you right now where I'll be and what I'll be doing this same time next year.*

- ❏ *I'm pretty sure about where I'm going. I could tell you what direction I'm going, but I've left room for opportunity.*

- ❏ *I take life as it comes. Who knows where I'll be three months from now? You never can tell what might happen between now and then.*

I love a good adventure as much as anyone, but I'm not willing to risk squandering my potential or not fulfilling my purpose by sitting back passively and letting things happen any old way. Life is not a dress rehearsal. We get one chance, and if we don't make the most of it, we can do nothing to get our time back and try again.

That's one of the reasons my wife, Margaret, and I are planners. We believe in preparation for many things in life, including taking a trip. We map out our whole itinerary because we already know about the places we want to go, the stores we want to shop, and even some of the places we want to eat.

Most travelers are only marginally organized when they take a trip. They usually get to the airport in their destination city, gather their luggage, try to get directions to their hotel, check in, get their belongings squared away, and rest up. Then they take time to think about what they want to do first. By the time they get started with the fun, they have already lost a big part of their day.

In contrast, when Margaret and I travel, we have a system where we split up the duties so that we can get out of any airport quickly. And while the other travelers from our flight are trying to figure out where to pick up their luggage, we're already halfway to our first sightseeing destination.

That kind of planning has always paid off. We make the most of every moment. Whenever we talk to our friends about places in common where we've traveled, we usually find that we've taken in most of the sights they have, plus a handful of other interesting places they wish they hadn't missed.

If planning can bring so many rewards, imagine the power of planning the success journey. Without planning, your progress in life will be like that of a Sunday driver, who may see a few interesting sights, but misses out on the truly incredible journey that could have been his.

TYPES OF "TRAVELERS"

Did you know that most people give more time to planning their vacations than they do to planning their lives? Based on the way people spend their planning time, you'd think they put in two weeks on the job each year and fifty on vacation. If you look at how people approach the planning process for the journey of life, I think you'll see that they fall into one of these categories:

- *Vince the Victim:* Vince is very quick to tell you that it's not his fault that he isn't getting anywhere in life. He doesn't make any plans because he is busy focusing his time and energy on things outside his control—often from his past. He frequently blames others for his lack of progress and seems to be more concerned with finding excuses for failing than with seizing opportunities to grow. In his opinion, everyone and everything other than himself has made him who he is today.

- *Foot-Dragging Freddie:* Freddie isn't worried too much about the past, and he doesn't want to think about the future. He is focused on the present. In fact, he loves the present so much that he is willing to do almost anything to maintain the status quo. He hates change and avoids it at all costs. If he is making any plans, they're to keep things the way they are.

- *Debbie the Dreamer:* Debbie loves to plan, and she spends a lot of her time doing that. The problem is that she never turns her plans into action. She often has great ideas and says she wants to be successful, but she doesn't want to take any risks. She is not willing to pay the price required to move forward on the success journey.

- *Motivated Michael:* Finally, there is Michael. He focuses the majority of his time on the present, doing his best to maximize his potential. But one reason he is so effective today is that he spent a portion of his time yesterday planning. As a result, he is focused on his purpose, he is growing toward his potential, and he is sowing seeds that benefit others out of the positive overflow in his life.

Which traveler do you most resemble: Michael, Debbie, Freddie, or Vince? How so?

_____

_____

_____

TAKE ACTION

Look at your calendar or day-planner for this year. Have you set goals for yourself? Have you noted the meetings, deadlines, and major events for the year? If not, take time today to plan out your year in as much detail as you can. If you don't have a calendar or day-planner that you work from, go buy one.

DAY 2

THE ROUTE

Take a moment to review the four travelers from yesterday's lesson.

What separates "Motivated Michael" from all the others?

_____

_____

_____

Michael has goals. He has identified what he wants to accomplish to fulfill his purpose and maximize his potential. You see, on the success journey, the goals you set become your route. And to make progress, you need that—not because you're hoping or expecting to reach some final destination, but because it shows you *how to take the journey*. On the success journey, the first part of the trip is just as important as the last part. The main thing is to be constantly moving *toward* your destination. And setting goals is the best way to make sure that continues to happen.

Think about what is involved in taking a long trip by car. Let's say, for example, you decide to go to Chicago from Dallas. If you've never taken that trip before, you wouldn't hop in the car and say, "I know Chicago is north of Dallas, so I'll take the first road I can find that goes north and start driving." That wouldn't make any sense at all. No, first you'd look at a map, consider the routes you could take, and decide on the best one, based on what kinds of roads you want to travel and what you'd like to see along the way.

The journey doesn't take care of itself. You have to plan it. If you just start driving, there is no telling where you'll end up. But when you plan ahead and know where you're going, you can successfully make the journey, and you can do it in good time and enjoy the trip along the way.

If you've been a member of an organization such as the American

Automobile Association (AAA), maybe you've asked them to help you plan a trip. You tell them your starting point and destination, and they plan out your route and give you a TripTik, a step-by-step map and guide showing you every town you need to drive through, where to change from one road to another, and what sights you can see along the way.

Taking the success journey requires the same attention to detail that a trip to Chicago would. It needs to be broken down into smaller segments to be more manageable. Goals are like points on a travel TripTik. Each one leads to the next and takes you farther in the right direction. Together, they set you on a course that leads toward your destination. And if you take a wrong turn along the way, you know it and can easily make adjustments to get back on track.

> *Describe a time when you've gotten off track. Would that experience have been different if you'd had a plan listing your goals that you could turn to? Or, if you did have a plan, how did that help you to get back on track?*

_____

_____

_____

I once heard a story about Supreme Court Justice Oliver Wendell Holmes that illustrates the importance of having a plan and knowing where you're going. According to the story, Holmes had misplaced his ticket while traveling on a train. He searched for it, obviously irritated, as the conductor stood by waiting. Finally, the train official told Holmes, "Your Honor, if you do not find your ticket, you can simply mail it to the railroad. We know and trust you."

Holmes replied, "I am not so concerned about your getting my ticket. I just want to know where I'm going."

Goals take care of that kind of problem because they make it possible for you to always know where you're going. With them, you will be able to fulfill your purpose in life and live your dream. Here are some of the ways goals do that.

GOALS AS GUIDES

GOALS DRAW OUT YOUR SENSE OF PURPOSE

The number of people today who lack a strong sense of purpose is astounding. Unfortunately, lack of direction seems to be growing, not decreasing. Pulitzer prize–winning writer Katherine Anne Porter observed, "I am appalled at the aimlessness of most people's lives. Fifty percent don't pay any attention to where they are going; forty percent are undecided and will go in any direction. Only ten percent know what they want, and even all of them don't go toward it."

How do your goals give you a sense of purpose?

_____

_____

_____

Goals give you something concrete to focus on, and that has a positive impact on your actions. As James Allen said, "You will become as small as your controlling desire, as great as your dominant aspiration." Goals help you focus your attention on your purpose and make it your dominant aspiration. They help you know where you're going. And as philosopher-poet Ralph Waldo Emerson wrote, "The world makes way for the man who knows where he is going."

GOALS GIVE YOU "GO"

Millionaire industrialist Andrew Carnegie said, "You cannot push anyone up the ladder unless he is willing to climb himself." The same is true of a person on the success journey: she won't go forward unless she is motivated to do so. Goals can help provide that motivation. Paul Myer commented, "No one ever accomplishes anything of consequence without a goal . . . Goal setting is the strongest human force for self-motivation."

How do your goals motivate you?

_____

_____

_____

Think about it. What is one of the greatest motivators in the world? Success. When you take a large activity (such as your dream) and break it down into smaller, more manageable parts (goals), you set yourself up for success because you make what you want to accomplish obtainable. And each time you accomplish a small goal, you experience success. That's motivating! Accomplish enough of the small goals, and you'll be taking a major step toward achieving your purpose and developing your potential.

Goals not only help you develop initial motivation by making your dreams obtainable, but they also help you continue to be motivated—and that creates momentum. Once you get going on the success journey, it will be very hard to stop you. The process is similar to what happens with a train. Getting it started is the toughest part of its trip. While standing still, a train can be prevented from moving forward by placing one-inch blocks of wood under each of the locomotive's drive wheels. Once a train gets up to speed, however, not even a steel-reinforced concrete wall five feet thick can stop it.

The link between goals and motivation is incredible. Your activities give you some pleasure, but sustaining them for any length of time is difficult. Setting and meeting goals, however, creates positive energy and motivates you to keep going even when obstacles arise.

GOALS SHOW YOU WHAT TO DO

All the motivation in the world is useless if it's wasted on things that don't matter. Goals help you to determine priorities, directing you to stick with what's important. How many successful people have you met who were unable to prioritize, who gave equal emphasis and energy to the trivial as well as the critical? I'd be willing to guess your answer is *none.* No one fulfills his purpose, develops his potential, or consistently helps others without goals. Your goals determine your priorities—and your priorities determine whether you'll reach your goals.

> *What did you spend time and energy on today that had nothing to do with reaching one of your goals?*

_____

_____

_____

Goals also keep your attention on the present. As English writer, poet, and politician Hilaire Belloc put it, "While you are dreaming of the future or regretting the past, the present, which is all you have, slips from you and is gone." To be successful, you must live and work in the present because that is where you have the power to actually accomplish something.

> *Name three things you did today that related to your goals.*

Action	Goal
_____	_____
_____	_____
_____	_____

GOALS GET YOUR FOCUS ON IMPROVEMENT, NOT ACTIVITY

As I've mentioned before, most unsuccessful people cling to the idea that success is a destination. By now, you're beginning to see that success truly is a journey. But don't allow that knowledge to make you believe that activity alone can make you successful. It doesn't. The real key to success and to reaching your potential lies in your ability to continually improve. Activity alone does nothing for you. It can distract you from reaching your potential if it becomes a substitute for improvement. But when you set the right goals and work to reach them instead of simply staying busy, improvement is not only obtainable—it's inevitable.

GOALS CREATE MILE MARKERS OF PROGRESS

I mentioned before that when you have goals, you are able to know quickly when you have gotten off track. Each time you reach a goal, you cannot only tell that you're making progress, but you can also see *how far* you have traveled. Goals are like mile markers on the success journey.

People have an innate need to know what kind of progress they're making. Margaret and I got to see a vivid example of this when we took a long flight together to Asia. While we were on the plane, the screens that ordinarily show movies and preflight safety information were used to project a large map of the world, and they showed the current position of our plane. As time went by, and we watched the little plane on the screen make its way across the Pacific Ocean, we had a visual reminder of how much progress we were making.

TAKE ACTION

Many times we work and work without really seeing how all of our actions go together to meet a goal. As an exercise, choose one of the projects you are working on right now. In the area below, list all of the steps or minigoals you will have to reach in order to complete the project. (Depending on the project size, you may need a separate sheet of paper.) As you complete each step, check it off.

_____

PROJECT GOAL

_____

STEP

_____

STEP

_____

STEP

DAY 3

FINDING YOUR PURPOSE

When you commit yourself to your dream and express it in achievable goals, you provide yourself with a visual reminder of where you're going and how you hope to get there. It's part of the success process:

> Your dream determines your goals.
> Your goals map out your actions.
> Your actions create results.
> And the results bring you success.

To make the success journey, you have to start with a dream. But that dream will become a reality only if you bridge the gap between intentions and actions by identifying a series of goals.

So how do you get started in the process of plotting goals on your Road Map for Success? Here are some instructions for determined travelers.

RECOGNIZE YOUR DREAM

Everything starts with your dream. It's an expression of your life purpose and determines what it means for you to reach your potential. If you can articulate your dream clearly, then you can create a map for your journey. If you can't, the trip will be nearly impossible. You won't be successful until you know where you want to go. As President Woodrow Wilson stated, "We grow by dreams."

OBSERVE YOUR STARTING PLACE

It's true that you can't begin the success journey until you know where you want to go. But you also can't be successful if you don't know where you're starting from—both pieces of information are necessary to make the trip. As Eric Hoffer, known as the "longshoreman philosopher," said, "To become *different* from what we are, we must have some *awareness* of what we are" (emphasis added).

Start by examining yourself as honestly as you can.

What are your three greatest talents/strengths?

_____

_____

_____

What have your unique life experiences prepared you to do? (education, trips, work experience, relationships)

_____

_____

_____

Name your current resources (including time, money, people, opportunities, etc.).

_____

_____

_____

Once you have a sense of where you are, ask yourself the following questions.

How Great a Distance Will I Have to Travel?

If your dream is to earn enough money to retire in ten years (as it was for my friend Paul Nanney), then you need to calculate exactly how much money you will need to earn to be able to achieve your goal. If your goal is to become a nurse or an engineer, then you need to contact universities to get information on programs of study, tuition costs, admission policies, and so on. No matter what you want to do, you will have to travel some distance to make it happen. You need to know how much ground you'll have to cover.

Describe the distance you will have to travel.

_____

WHAT DO I HAVE WORKING FOR ME?

No matter where you're starting from on your journey, you have some things going for you. If your dream is to own a business, a skill such as a knack for handling money will be an asset. If success to you means raising your children well, and you love kids and have the ability to teach, you're ahead of the game. Look for the things that are going to give you a head start. And don't just look at inherent abilities. Look at your circumstances, resources, and contacts.

Describe what you already have going for you.

_____

WHAT MUST I OVERCOME?

You will also have some things working against you. If your dream requires you to get a college degree but you have trouble reading, that's an obstacle you're going to have to overcome. If your desire is to play professional football, but you're only five feet, three inches tall and weigh 130 pounds, your physique is definitely going to work against you. No matter what your goal, hoping that your shortcomings will go away isn't going to help. You have to take an honest look at where you're starting and be prepared to overcome the obstacles.

Describe your obstacles.

_____

_____

WHAT WILL IT COST TO MAKE THE TRIP?

Every journey has costs associated with it. These costs may be in terms of time, energy, finances, choices, sacrifices, or a combination of factors. You will have to decide whether you're willing to pay that price. (We will look at this more in depth at Week 7.)

As you think about your dream and measure it against your starting place, you will be able to define it more precisely. You will begin to get a clearer picture of what's important to you and what you're willing to give—and to give up—to be successful. And you will be in a better position to identify specific goals.

ARTICULATE A STATEMENT OF PURPOSE

Once you've given more thought to your dream, and it has started to become clearer in your mind, you're ready to take another step: writing a statement of purpose for yourself based on your dream and what you intend to be doing while you're going in that direction. I guess you could call it your "philosophy of travel" for the success journey.

Begin with the general definition of success that I gave you in Week 1: success is knowing your purpose in life, growing to reach your maximum potential, and sowing seeds that benefit others. Then build on it. Your goal is to end up with a concise single statement that expresses what you want to do in your life. Your definition of success, your goals, and 80 percent of your daily activities should fall within the context of your purpose statement.

Here are a few purpose statements as examples so that you'll know what I mean:

Management expert Bob Buford: "My life mission is: to transform the latent energy in American Christianity into active energy."[1]

Attorney/writer Freyda Ottem Hansom: "To offer compassionate, complete, competent services in my law practice, to write words that inspire God-pleasing changes in others, and to make my life be such that I live to bless humankind."[2]

My personal writer/researcher Charlie Wetzel: "Through writing, teaching, and mentoring, I desire to inspire people to greatness by helping them discover their purpose, develop their relationship with God, and reach their potential."

TAKE ACTION

Your purpose statement should naturally grow out of your dreams, values, and convictions. So creating it isn't a quick, onetime event. Instead, most people develop and then refine it over the course of a couple of years. Spend time today writing yours. And remember not to expect perfection the first time around. Write it the best you can, and plan to make changes later as you discover more about yourself and refine the vision for your life.

My purpose is

_____

_____

_____

_____

DAY 4

DEFINING YOUR GOALS

Once you have articulated your purpose, you're ready to identify your goals—your points of reference on your road map. They will be activities or accomplishments that you plan to complete to fulfill your purpose, develop your potential, and help others. Use the following guidelines to keep your goals on target.

GOALS MUST BE . . .

WRITTEN

A goal properly set is halfway reached, and a goal written is set. The process of writing down goals helps you to clarify what you intend to do, to understand the importance of your goals, and to commit yourself to making them happen. Writing your goals also makes you more accountable.

PERSONAL

A common mistake is to identify something outside of your control as a goal. For instance, many people say their goal is to win the lottery. Or they say they want their spouses to treat them better. But they have no control over these things. To be legitimate, a goal must be within your power to achieve or accomplish personally. As you write each goal, make sure it passes the test.

SPECIFIC

The key to making a goal obtainable is to make it specific. Think about what would happen if you went into a restaurant and told your waiter, "I'd like food, please," when he took your order. There is no telling what you would get. The same is true when you set a goal. You have to spell out what you intend to do. And if a goal is big, break it down into smaller, more manageable tasks. You can't do what you can't express specifically.

ACHIEVABLE

Successful people set goals just out of reach, but not out of sight. University of South Carolina professor William Mobley said, "One of the most important things about golf is the presence of clear goals. You see the pins, you know the par—it's neither too easy nor unattainable, you know your average score, and there are competitive goals." As you identify your goals, you'll want to identify activities that will require you to work and stretch. But never put them so far out of your reach that you can't achieve them. You'll be discouraged by identifying a goal for yourself that you can't accomplish. Goals need to be motivating, not intimidating.

MEASURABLE

Goals have value only if they help you improve yourself and develop your potential. That's why they must be measurable. State your goals as objectively as possible so that you will be able to answer with a simple yes or no when you ask yourself the question, *Have I achieved this goal?*

> *Exercise: How could you restate the following goal so it would be measurable: "My goal is to be healthier." Rewrite it here.*

_____

_____

TIME-SENSITIVE

A goal has been called "a dream with a deadline." That's because without some kind of deadline, most goals never go from dream to reality. As you articulate each goal, write a completion date for it. If you don't, you can get into trouble. For example, if you've ever bought a house, you can imagine what might have happened if you had not set a date for closing the sale. You might have shown up with a moving van full of furniture only to find that the previous owners hadn't packed their first box. It would be a disaster. Setting a date for a real-estate transaction helps to ensure that you can take possession of your property on time. Likewise, attaching a date to each goal helps to ensure you will be able to take possession of it.

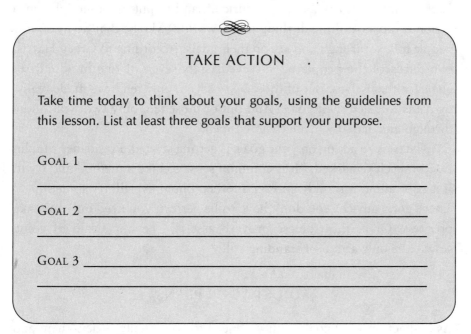

TAKE ACTION   .

Take time today to think about your goals, using the guidelines from this lesson. List at least three goals that support your purpose.

GOAL 1 _____

_____

GOAL 2 _____

_____

GOAL 3 _____

_____

DAY 5

AND . . . ACTION!

German poet and novelist Johann Wolfgang von Goethe once said, "Thinking is easy, acting is difficult, and to put one's thoughts into action is the most difficult thing in the world." Maybe that's why so few people follow through and act on their goals. According to Gregg Harris, two-thirds of the people he surveyed (sixty-seven of one hundred) set goals for themselves. But of those sixty-seven, only ten have made realistic plans to reach their goals. And out of those ten, only two will follow through and actually make them happen.[3]

The trick to acting on your goals is getting started. President Franklin D. Roosevelt remarked, "It is common sense to take a method and try it. If it fails, admit it frankly and try another. But above all, try something." That's good advice. You don't have to be perfect; you need only to make progress. Or as the Chinese proverb asserts, "Be not afraid of going slowly; be only afraid of standing still."

ADJUST YOUR PLANS

As you act on your goals, you will need to continually review them and your progress in order to make adjustments. Some goals won't really contribute to your dream or purpose and will need to be eliminated. Others will need to be modified. And in some cases, you'll simply fail. But as President Abraham Lincoln said, "My great concern is not whether you have failed, but whether you are content with your failure."

As you work on achieving your goals, think about this: although you should strive to write a purpose statement for yourself that will last a lifetime, you should plan to review and update goals on an almost continual basis.

When would be a logical time to review your goals?

_____

POINT TO SUCCESS AND CELEBRATE

Finally, as you accomplish some of your goals, take the time to celebrate. You deserve it. Acknowledge your successes, and build on them, always keeping in mind that your aim is not to achieve all your goals, but to improve constantly. Nobel prize–winning novelist William Faulkner urged, "Always dream and shoot higher than you know you can do. Don't bother just to be better than your contemporaries or predecessors. Try to be better than yourself." You're trying to fulfill your purpose, move toward your potential, and help others—not arrive at a destination.

What will you do to celebrate reaching one of your goals?

_____

Retail department store founder J. C. Penney declared, "Give me a stock clerk with a goal and I will give you a man who will make history. Give me a man without a goal and I will give you a stock clerk." Penney recognized the power and importance of goals. While you work on them, they work on you. And what you *get* by reaching your goals is not nearly as important as what you *become* by reaching them. In the case of Penney, he did more than become wealthy by building a chain of 1,600 retail stores with sales topping $4 billion. He developed his potential and that of others, giving generously to charities and helping the people who worked for him. After he took his company public in 1927, he gave shares of stock to all the managers in the company and included every employee in profit sharing. It's evident that he found his purpose, grew to his potential, and sowed seeds to benefit others. He truly was successful.

As you explore your dream, ponder your purpose, and identify your goals, be prepared for wonderful things to happen. There is no telling what will transpire on the success journey. Your life may ultimately exceed your expectations. But you have to begin somewhere to accomplish your dream, and setting goals is a great place to start.

CHARTING THE COURSE

Turn to "My Road Map for Success" in the back of the workbook and complete Section C under *Knowing My Purpose*.

Week

5

WHAT SHOULD I PACK IN MY SUITCASE?

PRINCIPAL QUESTIONS

DAY 1: When is my personal growth time?

DAY 2: When was the last time I did something that was outside of my comfort zone?

DAY 3: Am I dedicated to growing?

DAY 4: How can I ensure my continued personal growth?

DAY 5: What will I do each day to grow?

DAY 1

GETTING STARTED

Have you ever watched people pack for a long trip? It's amazing. Some run out the door without taking the essentials. Others, like my sister Trish, seem to pack the entire closet. I do a lot of traveling as a speaker, and it seems that I'm always preparing for a trip. During the last ten years, I've logged more than 2.5 million air miles—just on one airline. But I'm fortunate because Margaret helps me when I'm getting ready to leave for a trip. I usually let her know what kinds of speaking engagements and commitments I'm going to have, and she'll pack all my clothes and the other personal things I'll need.

How do you normally pack for a trip?

❑ *I put everything I can think of into suitcases. If I think of more things, I add more bags. You can never have enough stuff!*

❑ *First, I go over my itinerary and watch the weather report. Then I neatly lay out all the clothes and accessories that would be appropriate for the trip. If there are additional items I need, I make a list and go shopping for them. All items are neatly folded and packed in the order in which they will most likely be used. I'm done packing with time to spare.*

❑ *The morning of the trip I haphazardly rush to find clothes that are clean and toiletries that are usable. As I rush through the door to leave, I am grabbing three things that I forgot to pack.*

We all have different ways of packing for the trip, but I go through another packing process before I take any trip: I pack my briefcase. You see, I always work when I travel. I write, read, review reports, and do similar tasks. I'm always amazed when I get on a plane and start laying out my work and see a businessperson sitting next to me staring out the window. I can't believe he has nothing to do, and I'm always tempted to say, "Hey, since you're not busy, can I give you a couple of things to do for me before the plane lands in Dallas?"

Even without enlisting the help of others, I'm able to get a tremendous amount of work done on the road because I have a secret: I dedicate several hours to packing my briefcase before I leave on any trip. I study my itinerary to see what free blocks of time I'll have—during plane flights, at the end of the day in my hotel, between speaking engagements—and I check to see what work I need to get done for the upcoming weeks. Then I gather together all the materials I'll need for the trip: folders of notes and ideas I've collected for a lesson, quotes from my files, books and magazines I want to read and glean information from, reports I want to read, correspondence I want to answer.

The secret to making this system work is the time I spend *before* I leave. Since I started doing this, I've never been on the road and thought, *I could have gotten this project done or finished that lesson if only I had remembered to bring along such and such.*

> *What can you take along on your next trip? (Either work-related or for your personal growth.)*

_____

PACKING FOR THE SUCCESS JOURNEY

As you prepare to take the success journey, there is an essential activity that only you can perform for yourself. It's the equivalent of packing your briefcase for a trip because it determines what you will be capable of accomplishing on your journey. That activity is preparing and pursuing a personal growth plan. That process, more than anything else, will determine whether you will continue growing toward your maximum potential. And as the old Irish proverb says, "You've got to do your own growing, no matter how tall your grandfather is." In other words, nothing in your past guarantees that you will continue growing toward your potential in the future—not positions obtained, degrees earned, experience gained, awards received, or fortunes acquired. Planning your growth—and then following through with it—is the only thing that works.

A few years ago, while I was teaching a leadership conference, a man who was about sixty years old came up to me during a break and said, "I'm learning so much at this conference. I wish I had heard you twenty years ago!"

I smiled and said, "No, you don't. You wouldn't have wanted to listen to me twenty years ago."

"Why do you say that?" he asked.

"Twenty years ago," I answered, "I didn't have anything to say. I didn't know these things. Everything I'm sharing with you this morning has come as a result of years of continual learning and growth."

The desire and discipline to keep growing have always been very important to me. When I was growing up, my dad put me on a reading plan. Every day he required me to read for thirty minutes out of books he selected. And when I got my very first driver's license, Dad put a book in the glove compartment of the car and said, "Son, never travel anywhere without a book. If you get stuck, you can use the time to read and improve yourself." Dad also sent me to seminars, such as Dale Carnegie's "How to Win Friends and Influence People," when I was still in high school.

My dad's growth plan sure helped me learn the value of personal growth, and when I was seventeen, I took a more active role in my development. That's when I began to read systematically and file outstanding quotes from books and magazines. I had learned that shortcuts don't pay off in the long run. If I was going to have a chance to reach my potential, I was going to have to keep learning, growing, and improving.

TAKE ACTION

Plan your growth time. Figure out exactly where you can "steal" an hour a day (five days a week). Do you need to make time—get up an hour earlier or maybe use your lunch hour to read or study? Or do you already have time—when you're waiting on others or traveling? Where you get the time is up to you, but be specific, write it on your calendar, and try to stick with your plan.

DAY 2

INITIATING CHANGE

The poet Robert Browning wrote, "Why stay we on the earth except to grow?" Just about anyone would agree that growing is a good thing, but relatively few people dedicate themselves to the process. Why? Because it requires change, and most people are reluctant to change. But the truth is that without change, growth is impossible. Author Gail Sheehy asserted,

> If we don't change, we don't grow. If we don't grow, we are not really living. Growth demands a temporary surrender of security. It may mean a giving up of familiar but limiting patterns, safe but unrewarding work, values no longer believed in, relationships that have lost their meaning. As Dostoevsky put it, "Taking a new step, uttering a new word, is what most people fear most." The real fear should be the opposite course.

I can't think of anything worse than living a stagnant life, devoid of change and improvement.

Why is growth impossible without change?

_____

_____

_____

GROWTH IS A CHOICE

Most people fight against change, especially when it affects them personally. As novelist Leo Tolstoy said, "Everyone thinks of changing the world, but no one thinks of changing himself." The ironic thing is that change is inevitable. Everybody has to deal with it. On the other hand, growth is optional. You can choose to grow or fight it. But know this: People unwilling to grow will *never* reach their potential.

In one of his books, my friend Howard Hendricks asks the question, "How have you changed . . . lately? In the last week, let's say? Or the last month? The last year? Can you be *very specific*?" He knows how people tend to get into a rut when it comes to growth and change. Growth is a choice, a decision that can really make a difference in a person's life.

Answer Howard's question: How have you changed lately? (be specific)

In the last week: _____

In the last month: _____

In the last year: _____

Most people don't realize that successful and unsuccessful people do not differ substantially in their abilities. They vary in their desire to reach their potential. And nothing is more effective when it comes to reaching potential than commitment to personal growth.

LET ME HELP YOU PACK

Making the change from being an occasional learner to becoming someone dedicated to personal growth goes against the grain of the way most people live. If you asked one hundred people how many books they have read on their own since leaving school, I bet only a handful would say they have read more than one or two books. If you asked how many listen to tapes and voluntarily attend conferences and seminars to grow personally, there would be even fewer. Most people celebrate when they receive their diploma or degree and say to themselves, "Thank goodness that's over. Just let me have a good job. I'm finished with studying." But such thinking doesn't take you any higher than average. If you want to take the success journey, you have to keep growing.

As someone who has dedicated his life to personal growth and development, I'd like to help you make the leap to becoming a dedicated self-developer. It's the way you need to go if you want to reach your potential. Besides that, it also has another benefit: it brings contentment. The happiest people I know are growing every day.

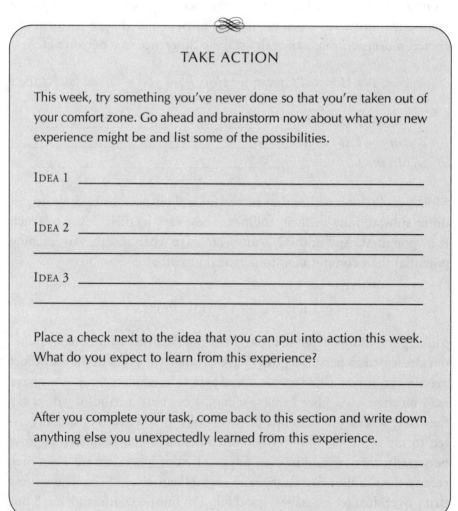

TAKE ACTION

This week, try something you've never done so that you're taken out of your comfort zone. Go ahead and brainstorm now about what your new experience might be and list some of the possibilities.

IDEA 1 _____

_____

IDEA 2 _____

_____

IDEA 3 _____

_____

Place a check next to the idea that you can put into action this week. What do you expect to learn from this experience?

_____

After you complete your task, come back to this section and write down anything else you unexpectedly learned from this experience.

_____

_____

DAY 3

MAKING CHOICES

It's said that when Spanish composer-cellist Pablo Casals was in the final years of his life, a young reporter asked him, "Mr. Casals, you are ninety-five years old and the greatest cellist who ever lived. Why do you still practice six hours a day?"

What was Casals's answer? "Because I think I'm making progress." That's the kind of dedication to continual growth that you should have. The people who reach their potential, no matter what their profession or background, think in terms of improvement.

CHOOSE A LIFE OF GROWTH

If you think you can "hold your ground" and still make the success journey, you are mistaken. You need to have an attitude like that of General George Patton. It's said that he told his troops, "There is one thing I want you to remember. I don't want to get any messages saying, 'We are holding our position.' We are advancing constantly." Patton's motto was, "Always take the offensive. Never dig in."

The only way to improve the quality of your life is to improve yourself. If you want to grow your organization, you must grow as a leader. If you want to have better children, you must become a better person. If you want others to treat you more kindly, you must develop better people skills. There is no sure way to make other people or your environment improve. The only thing you truly have the ability to improve is yourself. And the amazing thing is that when you do, everything else around you suddenly gets better. So the bottom line is that if you want to take the success journey, you must live a life of growth. And the only way you *will* grow is if you *choose* to grow.

How can you improve in each of the following areas?

Family: _____

Relationships: _____

Career: _____

*Character:*_____

START GROWING TODAY

Napoleon Hill said, "It's not what you are going to do, but it's what you are doing now that counts." Many unsuccessful people have what I call "someday sickness." They could do some things to bring value to their lives right now, but they put them off and say they'll do them *someday*. Their motto is, "One of these days." But as the old English proverb says, "*One* of these days means *none* of these days." The best way to ensure success is to start growing today. No matter where you may be starting from, don't be discouraged—every person who got where he is started where he was.

> *When it comes to personal growth, what have you been putting off? Where should you focus your growth?*

_____

Why do you need to determine to start growing today? There are several reasons.

GROWTH IS NOT AUTOMATIC

In my book *Breakthrough Parenting*, I mention that you can be young only once, but you can be immature indefinitely.[1] That's because growth is not automatic. Just because you grow older doesn't mean you keep growing. That's how it is with some creatures, such as crustaceans. As a crab or a lobster ages, it grows and has to shed its shell. But that's not the trend for people. The road to the next level is uphill, and it takes effort to keep growing. The sooner you start, the closer to reaching your potential you'll be.

GROWTH TODAY WILL PROVIDE A BETTER TOMORROW

Everything you do today builds on what you did yesterday. And altogether, those things determine what will happen tomorrow. That's especially true in regard to growth. Oliver Wendell Holmes offered this insight: "Man's mind, once stretched by a new idea, never regains its original dimensions." Growth today is an investment for tomorrow.

GROWTH IS YOUR RESPONSIBILITY

When you were a small child, your parents were responsible for you—even for your growth and education. But as an adult, you bear that responsibility entirely. If you don't *make* growth your responsibility, it will never happen.

There is no time like right now to get started. Recognize the importance that personal growth plays in success, and commit yourself to developing your potential today.

BE TEACHABLE

Former UCLA basketball coach John Wooden is an inspiring model of personal growth. He continually developed himself, and he did the same with his players, trying to help them reach their potential. One of my favorite sayings from him is this: "It's what you learn *after* you know it all that counts." Wooden recognized that the greatest obstacle to growth isn't ignorance—it's knowledge. The more you learn, the greater the chance you'll think you know it all. If that happens, you become unteachable, and you are no longer growing—or improving. When you remain teachable, your potential is almost limitless.

TAKE ACTION

True success always includes others. To get started with your personal growth plan, find a mentor. Pair up with someone you know who is growing and who has the most expertise in the area in which you'd most like to grow. Your goal is to develop a win-win relationship with that person, where both you and your mentor benefit from the relationship.

STAYING FOCUSED

There has been a change in focus over the last thirty years in the area of personal growth. Beginning in the late sixties and early seventies, people began talking about "finding themselves," meaning that they were searching for a way to become self-fulfilled. It's like making happiness a goal, because self-fulfillment is about feeling good.

But self-development is different. Sure, most of the time it will make you feel good, but that's a by-product, not the goal. Self-development is a higher calling; it is the development of your potential so that you can attain the purpose for which you were created. There are times when that's fulfilling, but other times it's not. No matter how it makes you feel, self-development always has one effect: it draws you toward your destiny. Rabbi Samuel M. Silver taught, "The greatest of all miracles is that we need not be tomorrow what we are today, but we can improve if we make use of the potential implanted in us by God."

Up to now, have you been more focused on self-fulfillment or self-development? Why? How can you change to strengthen your focus?

_____

_____

_____

NEVER STAY SATISFIED WITH
CURRENT ACCOMPLISHMENTS

My friend Rick Warren says, "The greatest enemy of tomorrow's success is today's success." He is right. Thinking that you have "arrived" when you accomplish a goal has the same effect as believing you know it all. It takes away your desire to learn. It's another characteristic of destination disease. But successful people don't sit back and rest on their laurels. They know that wins—like losses—are temporary, and they have to keep growing if they want to continue being successful. Charles Handy remarked, "It is one of the paradoxes of success that the things and ways which got you there are seldom those things that keep you there."

No matter how successful you are today, don't get complacent. Stay hungry. Sydney Harris insisted, "A winner knows how much he still has to learn, even when he is considered an expert by others; a loser wants to be considered an expert by others before he has learned enough to know how little he knows." Don't settle into a comfort zone, and don't let success go to your head. Enjoy your success briefly, and then move on to greater growth.

Using an example from your own life, explain how "the greatest enemy of tomorrow's success can be today's success."

_____

_____

_____

BE A CONTINUAL LEARNER

The best way to keep from becoming satisfied with your current achievements is to make yourself a continual learner. That kind of commitment may be rarer than you realize. For example, a study performed by the University of Michigan several years ago found that one-third of all physicians in the United States are so busy working that they're two years behind the breakthroughs in their own fields.[2]

If you want to be a continual learner and keep growing throughout your life, you'll have to carve out the time to do it. You'll have to do what you can wherever you are. As Henry Ford said, "It's been my observation that most successful people get ahead during the time other people waste."

That's one reason I carry books and magazines with me whenever I travel. During the downtimes, such as waiting for a connection in an airport, I can go through a stack of magazines, reading and cutting out articles. Or I can skim a book, learning the major concepts and pulling out quotes I'll be able to use later. And when I'm in town, I maximize my learning time by continually listening to instructive tapes in the car.

Frank A. Clark stated, "Most of us must learn a great deal every day in order to keep ahead of what we forget." Learning something every day is the essence of being a continual learner. You must keep improving yourself, not only acquiring knowledge to replace what you forget or what's out of date, but also building on what you learned yesterday.

> *What did you learn today? Did you take advantage of any learning opportunities? What learning opportunities did you miss?*

_____

_____

_____

Dedication to growth not only enlarges you and increases your potential; it also motivates you. It begins a cycle of growth that, if sustained, leads to further and more extensive growth. And that leads to a more fulfilling and productive life. Dr. Charles Garfield, who has written about achievers, says this:

> Peak performers do not see accomplishment as a fixed state, nor as a safe haven in which the individual is moored, completed, finished. Not once have I heard a peak performer speak of an end to challenge, excitement, curiosity, and wonder. Quite the contrary. One of their most engaging characteristics is an infectious talent for moving into the future, generating new challenges, living with a sense of more work to be done.
>
> And they also live with a sense of more growth to be experienced.

During the course of my life, I've experienced the incredible power that regular personal growth brings. Week 3 showed you that attitude determines how far you can go in life. Growth adds another dimension to your abilities; it determines how well equipped you are for the journey. When your "suitcase" is packed well through continual personal development, you can go farther more quickly than you've ever dreamed, and the journey goes more smoothly because you're better prepared for it. Even when you face obstacles, which we'll talk about next week, you're better equipped to keep going.

TAKE ACTION

Turn back to Day 4 of Week 1 and look at the list of books, newspapers, and magazines you created. How can you incorporate these resources, along with lessons or books on tape, into your routine so you can be a continual learner? Look for any time that you might have in the weeks ahead. Example: time alone in the car, time between flights or on a flight, or time between projects. As a rule, make sure you always have something to either read or listen to when you are traveling.

DEDICATING YOURSELF TO GROWTH

It takes time to learn how to pack your suitcase. In the beginning, we all have a tendency to try to take too much with us—not only on the success journey, but also on the other trips we take as well. For example, a trip to Japan that Margaret and I took about fifteen years ago turned out to be a disaster because we didn't know how to pack. We bought two huge suitcases, and we filled them until they were absolutely full. We had done some traveling before, so we thought we were being smart by having only two heavy bags rather than a bunch of small ones. We would use porters or rental cars as we had done before at airports.

Everything was fine until we started trying to get around in Japan. A taxi delivered us to the train station in Tokyo, and after it dropped us off, we looked for a porter, but we couldn't find one. "No problem," I said. "I'll get one of those carts." We couldn't find one of those either. We ended up carrying those huge suitcases all over the station looking for the right track for our departure. Then we had to lug them onto the train and stow them away in our car.

We ended up doing that all over Japan. In one city, as we dragged the bags "only a short walk from the train station" to our hotel, I dropped them in the middle of the street and shouted, "If somebody wants these bags, come get 'em. I'll take five bucks for both of them—contents and all." There were no takers. But one good thing came out of that whole experience. Margaret and I learned our lesson on that trip, and since then, we have become very good packers.

When you learn to become a good packer on the success journey, you'll be surprised by how high you'll be able to climb. The key is to focus on what you need and not anything else. I've already shared with you the areas where I concentrate my personal development: relationships, attitude, communication, leadership, and personal growth. When I started working in those areas, my only goal was to improve myself. I wanted to become a better person, a more effective pastor, and a stronger leader. I wanted to develop myself in order to come closer to reaching my potential.

But my dedication has brought other benefits that I never hoped for. My goal wasn't to become an author or national speaker, but out of the overflow of the growth I've experienced, I have had the privilege of sharing what I've learned with others. Starting about twenty-five years ago, people began asking me to share what I've learned, and those requests keep increasing. I know that the only way I will be able to continue helping others is to keep learning and growing every day.

> *Write down one long-term goal that you have. Now, what must you do daily for the next several years to achieve that goal? Write it here.*

_____

_____

_____

If you dedicate yourself to personal development, there is no telling where it will lead you in life, but I know one thing for certain: it can take you only up. If you haven't already, get started today. Make growth your main goal, and be prepared to climb higher than you believed possible.

CHARTING THE COURSE

Turn to "My Road Map for Success" in the back of the workbook and complete Section A under *Growing to Reach My Maximum Potential.*

Week

6

HOW DO I HANDLE THE DETOURS?

DAY 1
Speed Bumps, Potholes, and Detours

DAY 2
The Two Greatest Detours

DAY 3
Face Your Fear

DAY 4
The Power of Failure

DAY 5
Failing Forward

PRINCIPAL QUESTIONS

DAY 1: How can I make the best of the detours and interruptions in my life?

DAY 2: Am I allowing fear to control my life?

DAY 3: How can I actively face my fear?

DAY 4: What is the right attitude toward failure?

DAY 5: How can I fail forward?

DAY 1

SPEED BUMPS, POTHOLES, AND DETOURS

When you take a journey, you never know for sure whether it will turn out the way you planned—a lot can happen along the way that you don't expect. That's what happened to Margaret and me on the way home from a trip to the Holy Land a few years ago. We have been to Israel several times, and on that particular trip we took fifty people with us for a tour. Margaret and I are superplanners, so in the space of a week, we saw more sights than many thought was humanly possible. By the time we were headed back home, everyone was exhausted.

When we arrived in Paris from Tel Aviv at midmorning an agent from the airline greeted us. "I'm sorry, folks," she said, "but your flight to New York has been canceled. There's a major snowstorm on the Atlantic Coast, and nothing is going in or out for the next twenty-four hours." After a week of being on dusty roads, rushing from sight to sight, sleeping in strange hotel rooms, and seeing tense soldiers with machine guns everywhere, our group was ready to be back home.

As we got the news, I could sense the disappointment and frustration among our people. Many who were traveling with us were older and had never been out of the United States before. Previous departures from the planned itinerary had upset some of them. This major break in our travel plans was likely to send them into a panic.

Margaret and I looked at each other and knew we needed to act.

"Okay, gang, let's all get together over here," I said as I gathered everyone into a corner in the airport and took a quick head count. "How many of you have never been to Paris before?" I asked. All but a few hands went up. "Oh, this is great! We've got an awesome opportunity here," I explained. "We're going to take a tour of the city!"

Margaret's eyes lit up as she understood the idea, and she jumped right in to help. "Oh, you'll love Paris," she said. "It's the most romantic city in the world." A couple of the women in the group smiled, but the majority of the group looked at us with skepticism. "We'll see the Louvre, Notre Dame, the Eiffel Tower—you name it."

"We are so lucky," I said. "Do you know how much money most people spend to see Paris? They spend thousands of dollars just to get here, but we're going to see it for free." That got the attention of a couple of the men.

An hour later, we were at the hotel, and Margaret and I were working on getting the tour together. "No, monsieur," the concierge said, "there are no tours available. I can maybe arrange something for tomorrow."

"It has to be today. There must be something available," I said.

"No, monsieur. I am sorry."

"Then how about a bus?" said Margaret.

He looked at her blankly.

"Surely there's a bus in all of Paris. See if you can find us a bus—any kind of bus—and a driver."

"That's right," I agreed. "Just find us a bus. We don't care where you get it or what it looks like. It can be a school bus for all we care. We'll take care of the tour ourselves." It took us a while to convince him, but he finally agreed to try. And he got us a bus—complete with a driver who didn't speak a word of English.

We loaded up the group and gave them a whirlwind tour of Paris. "Take lots of pictures," we kept telling them. "You'll want to show everyone when you get home how you got an extra trip to Paris." We showed them everything we could. And I'll bet we even got the landmarks' names right, oh, 70 or 80 percent of the time. They experienced things they wouldn't have on another tour. For instance, we spotted pop singer Madonna coming out of the Louvre surrounded by bodyguards, and everyone took pictures of her.

"It could happen only on the Maxwell tour," one member of the group said later.

After we got home, our people had meaningful memories of Israel and the awe-inspiring places there. But their favorite story was about their one-day side trip to Paris.

Have you ever been on a trip that didn't turn out the way you planned? If you've done much traveling, maybe I should ask instead if you've ever been on a trip that *did* turn out exactly as you planned. Because if you're like most people, you've had all kinds of things go wrong on a trip. The success journey is the same way. You may have your journey clearly marked on your road map, but until you are actually traveling, the obstacles are not apparent. The journey is full of speed bumps, potholes, and detours. And since nobody can entirely avoid them, the question is, How are you handling them?

Describe how you typically respond to the potholes and detours on your journey.

_____

_____

_____

TAKE ACTION

Find one example of a leader who experienced a detour on his or her journey and was successful in spite of the challenge. What was his attitude toward the challenge? What actions did he take in order to move on?

DAY 2

THE TWO GREATEST DETOURS

As I've talked to people about success, I've found that the two greatest detours they face are fear and failure. When you think about it, those two deterrents could have stopped our tour group from having a good time in Paris. Fear of the unknown could have kept us huddled in the airport instead of heading out and enjoying the city. And nobody could have blamed us if we had given up when we experienced our first failure—not being able to find a bus tour. But fear and failure didn't stop us. Neither should they stop you from taking the success journey. You see, every detour is also a potential opportunity, and it can prevent you from being successful only if you let it.

FACTS ABOUT FEAR

All people experience fear; it's a part of life. *What* we fear may change with the times, but every generation experiences it. Look at these quotes from the last 379 years and you'll recognize a common theme. In 1623, Sir Francis Bacon said, "Nothing is terrible except for fear itself." About two hundred years later, the Duke of Wellington declared, "The only thing I am afraid of is fear." And more recently, our own Franklin D. Roosevelt asserted, "The only thing we have to fear is fear itself."

We all have fears. Nine out of ten people are terrified by the thought of speaking before groups. Some don't like insects. Others fear heights, deep water, financial problems, aging, or loneliness. Fears come in almost as many varieties as people do.

What are some of your everyday fears? List them below.

_____

_____

The fears of some well-known people from history are comical. For example, Julius Caesar, a powerful military general and Roman emperor, feared thunder. Peter the Great, the czar of Russia and an imposing figure at six feet, five inches tall, was afraid of bridges. He crossed them only when there was no other alternative, and when he did, he trembled and cried like a child. And eighteenth-century British writer and literary critic Dr. Samuel Johnson had a phobia about entering a room with his left foot. Any time he accidentally entered a room wrong-footed, he backed out and entered again. He took wanting to put his best foot forward to a ridiculous extreme.

THE FALLOUT OF FEAR

No matter how foolish or humorous another person's fears may look to us, our own seem serious. One reason is that fear can be a hindrance to success. If allowed to control our lives, fear can be a permanent detour on the success journey, stopping us from making any progress. Ironically, when fear succeeds in preventing us from engaging in an activity, we never find out whether that fear was truly justifiable. And that creates a vicious cycle, which can eventually take over our lives. Take a look at the pattern fear can create in a person's life:

Fear breeds *inaction;*
Inaction leads to *lack of experience;*
Lack of experience fosters *ignorance;* and
Ignorance breeds *fear.*

How might your fears stand in the way of your next step on the success journey?

_____

_____

_____

President John F. Kennedy said, "There are risks and costs to a program of action, but they are far less than the long-range risks and costs of comfortable inaction." The bottom line is that if you can overcome your fear, you can break the cycle and live to see the death of your ignorance and the birth of your success.

Fear also causes procrastination. It divides our focus and weakens us. It can even make us feel isolated. Michael Pritchard called fear "that little darkroom where negatives are developed." And former NFL quarterback Fran Tarkenton said, "Fear causes people to draw back from situations; it brings on mediocrity; it dulls creativity; it sets one up to be a loser in life." Fear robs us of our potential and prevents us from moving forward toward our purpose in life.

How do you tend to deal with fear?

❑ *Avoid the things, people, and places that I'm afraid of.*

❑ *Hope that the fear will just go away on its own.*

❑ *Face up to them.*

FACE YOUR FEARS

When it comes to dealing with fear, you have three choices. First, you can try to avoid it altogether. But that means staying away from every known or potentially fear-producing person, place, thing, or situation. That's neither practical nor productive. If you move tentatively from place to place, always worrying that around the next corner you'll come face-to-face with something that could cause you to fear, you will be tied into knots.

A second way to deal with fear is to hope that it will go away. But that's like hoping for a fairy godmother to rescue you.

Fortunately, there is a third way to deal with fear, and that is to face it and overcome it. In the end, that's the only method that really works. Here is a strategy to help you face the fear and do it anyway.

DISCOVER THE FOUNDATION OF FEAR

Most of the fears we face every day are not based on facts. They are generated by our feelings. For example, a study conducted by the University of Michigan showed the following:

- 60 percent of our fears are totally unwarranted; they never come to pass.

- 20 percent of our fears are focused on our past, which is completely out of our control.

- 10 percent of our fears are based on things so petty that they make no difference in our lives.

- Of the remaining 10 percent, only 4 to 5 percent could be considered justifiable.

These statistics show that any time or energy you give to fear is totally wasted and counterproductive 95 percent of the time.[1]

What category do more of your fears fall into?

❑ *I fear things that will most likely never happen.*

❑ *My fears are a result of my past.*

❑ *I fear things that are trivial.*

TAKE ACTION

Fear is interest paid on a debt you may not owe. If you've allowed yourself to be detoured by unjustified fear, it's time to look beyond your feelings and examine the thinking that's generating your fears. Compare your thought patterns to the facts and see where they don't match up. If your focus is on the past, try to work through it and move on. You can't change the past, so don't dwell on it. If you're worrying about petty things, remind yourself of what is really important. And if you can't change your thought patterns on your own, seek the help of a professional counselor. Don't allow yourself to remain a prisoner of your feelings.

DAY 3

FACE YOUR FEAR

After you have dealt with all of your unjustifiable fears, there still may be a few justifiable fears remaining. And the best thing to do in the case of your few justifiable fears is to acknowledge them and keep moving forward. That's what our esteemed heroes have done. For example, consider the life and career of someone like George S. Patton, a bold and innovative general who was instrumental in the success of the Allies in World War II. You might be tempted to think that he didn't experience fear. But that's not the case. He felt the fear, but he didn't let it stop him. He once said, "I am not a brave man. The truth of the matter is I am usually a coward at heart. I have never been in the sound of gunshot or sight of battle in my whole life that I was not afraid. I constantly have sweat on my palms and a lump in my throat." Imagine that: one of our bravest generals thought of himself as a coward.

One key to Patton's success was that he learned how to deal with his fear. He declared, "The time to take counsel of your fears is before you make an important battle decision. That's the time to listen to every fear you can imagine. When you have collected all the facts and fears and made your decision, turn off all of your fears and go ahead!" If someone who considered himself a coward could do that, so can you.

MORE STRATEGIES FOR COMBATING FEAR

ACCEPT FEAR AS THE PRICE OF PROGRESS

You must realize that the things you fear will come true or they won't. And your fear will not positively affect the outcome. Fear can only detour you—if you let it. That's why it's critical to accept fear as the price of progress. Dr. Susan Jeffries admitted, "As long as I continue to stretch my capabilities, as long as I continue to make risks in making my dreams come true, I am going to experience fear."

Any time you try to move forward into new territory on the success journey, there is a chance that you will fail. Your attempt to move forward may also make you look foolish. And the thought of that probably makes you nervous. That's all right. Just about every person who ever achieved something of value faced fear and moved forward anyway. True heroes are the men and women who conquer themselves.

Write a credo to help you face and overcome your fears in the future.

_____
_____
_____
_____

DEVELOP A BURNING DESIRE

Your dream is one of the most effective antidotes for fear. It can fuel the flames of desire within you until you're willing to confront and overcome your fear. Your dream can help you go where you're afraid to go and do what you're afraid to do. It will enable you to channel your fear positively. As professional boxing manager Cus D'Amato put it, "The hero and the coward both feel exactly the same fear, only the hero confronts his fear and converts it into fire." Your dream can provide the spark that will turn your fear into fire.

What is your dream? _____

Fear	*How can I turn it into fire?*
_____	_____
_____	_____
_____	_____
_____	_____
_____	_____

FOCUS ON THINGS YOU CAN CONTROL

Former UCLA basketball coach John Wooden, one of the greatest coaches who ever lived, said, "Do not let what you cannot do interfere with what you can do." As you move forward on the success journey, you need to remember that what happens *in* you is more important than what happens *to* you. You can control your attitudes as you travel on the journey, but you have no control over the actions of others. You can choose what to put on your calendar, but you can't control today's circumstances. Unfortunately, the majority of the fear and stress that people experience in life is from things they can do nothing about. Don't let that happen to you.

List the things you can and cannot control concerning your fear:

Things I Can Control   *Things I Cannot Control*

_____   _____

_____   _____

_____   _____

Determine to accept what you cannot control and release it.

PUT SOME WINS UNDER YOUR BELT

Vince Lombardi, legendary coach of the NFL's Green Bay Packers, once commented, "Winning is a habit. Unfortunately, so is losing." He understood that past successes influence the ability to perform well. That principle also applies to overcoming fears. Each time you face a fear and move forward in spite of it, you are better prepared to challenge the next one. In time, you develop the habit of winning over fear, the smaller victories paving the way for the greater ones. Eventually, fear is no longer a major problem and no longer sends you on unnecessary detours from the success journey.

Make a list of the fears you have already overcome.

_____

_____

_____

FEED YOUR FAITH, NOT YOUR FEAR

The bottom line is that you have a choice. You can feed your fears, or you can starve them. Both fear and faith will be with you every minute of every day. But the emotion that you continually act upon—the one you feed—dominates your life. Acting on the right emotion lifts you to success, while acting on the wrong one starts you on a disheartening detour.

Feeling the fear and moving ahead anyway depends on changing your thought patterns from "Fear means stop" to "Fear means go." Mark Twain urged, "Do something every day that you don't want to do. This is the golden rule for acquiring the habit of doing your duty without pain."

The irony is that the successful person who keeps growing, taking risks, and moving forward feels the same feelings of fear as the one who allows fear to stop him. The difference comes because one doesn't let fear dominate while the other does.

TAKE ACTION

Give yourself a deadline to actively face your fear.

I will start working on my fear of _____
on (date) _____

To overcome this fear I will

_____

_____

DAY 4

THE POWER OF FAILURE

A few years ago, my friend Max Lucado visited me. He wanted to sharpen his leadership skills, and he asked me to give him a hand. So he came for the weekend, and we had a wonderful time. Max is an incredible writer—one of the finest Christian writers today. As we ate dinner one night, I asked him about getting his first book published.

"Well," he said, "in the beginning, nobody wanted to publish my stuff."

I almost choked on my food. "What?" I said. "What do you mean?" Max's prose reads like poetry. It's beautiful.

"Nobody wanted to publish it," he repeated. "I sent my first manuscript out to at least fifteen publishers before one finally said yes."

"I bet some of those publishers are kicking themselves now," I said. Max has published a lot of books since then, and has sold millions of copies. "When you were trying to get that first one accepted, didn't you ever get discouraged and think about giving up?"

"No," he said. "Every time I got the manuscript back, I thought, *Well, I'll just try another publisher.*"

That's when it hit me. Max had something that just about all successful people have: the ability to fail.

"Wait a minute!" you may be saying. "I thought we were talking about creating a Road Map for Success. Doesn't success mean avoiding failure?" The answer is no. All of us fail. As we travel, we all hit potholes, take wrong turns, or forget to check the radiator. The only person who avoids failure altogether is the person who never leaves his driveway. So the real issue is not whether you're going to fail. It's whether you're going to fail successfully (profiting from your failure) or allow failure to send you on a permanent detour. As Nelson Boswell observed, "The difference between greatness and mediocrity is often how an individual views mistakes." If you want to continue on the success journey, you need to learn to fail forward.

Why is it important to learn how to fail?

_____

_____

USE FAILURE AS A SPRINGBOARD

Unsuccessful people are often so afraid of failure and rejection that they spend their whole lives avoiding risks or decisions that could lead to failure. They don't realize that success is based on their ability to fail and continue trying. When you have the right attitude, failure is neither fatal nor final. In fact, it can be a springboard to success. Leadership expert Warren Bennis interviewed seventy of the nation's top performers in various fields and found that none of them viewed their mistakes as failures. When talking about them, they referred to their "learning experiences," "tuition paid," "detours," and "opportunities for growth."[2]

In the past, how would you have described your failures?

_____

Successful people don't let failure go to their heads. Instead of dwelling on the negative consequences of failure, thinking of what might have been and how things haven't worked out, they focus on the rewards of success: learning from their mistakes and thinking about how they can improve themselves and their situations. Depending on your attitude toward it, failure can either bog you down or help you along on your journey.

HOW TO FAIL FORWARD

Perhaps this isn't the first time you've heard this perspective on failure. Maybe you're willing to acknowledge the possibilities that this approach can offer, but you've had a tough time living it out.

Who is your favorite athlete and why?

_____

_____

_____

What kinds of setbacks has he or she had to overcome?

_____

Most of us have been conditioned to look only at the end result of any person's long success journey. For example, we celebrate when the Olympic Gold Medal goes to someone such as Jackie Joyner-Kersee, but we don't think about the many races and events she has lost over the years, the adjustments and relearning she has had to do to correct her technique, or the excruciating injuries she has sustained along the way.

It's time to change your thinking about failure and approach it in an entirely different way. With each failure, you can move one step farther on the success journey. As hotel executive Conrad Hilton put it, "Successful people keep moving. They make mistakes, but they don't quit."

CHANGE FAILURE FROM DETOUR TO DIVIDEND

There are ten guidelines to help you. Today we will look at the first five.

1. APPRECIATE THE VALUE OF FAILURE

Never forget that you cannot take the success journey without experiencing failure. In fact, train yourself to think of failures as mileage markers. Each time you fail, know that you've traveled another mile farther on the road to your potential. Soichino Honda, founder of Honda Motors, offered this insight: "Many people dream of success. To me success can be achieved only through repeated failure and introspection. In fact, success only represents one percent of your work that results from 90 percent of that which is called failure. Very few unacquainted with failure will ever know the true joy of success." I would go even further and say that no person unacquainted with failure will know success.

Failure has another value: it strengthens you. Henry Ward Beecher, nineteenth-century author, clergyman, and outspoken opponent to slavery, said, "It is defeat that turns bone to flint, and gristle to muscle, and makes people invincible, and formed those heroic natures that are now in ascendancy in the world. Do not, then, be afraid of defeat. You are never so near to victory as when defeated in a good cause." Each time you experience a fumble, failure, or defeat, remind yourself that you're one step closer to your potential and your dream. You're learning to fail forward to success.

On your own journey, how has failure moved you closer to your goal?

_____

_____

_____

2. Don't Take Failure Personally

Most people never learn to fail forward because they take failure personally. They start saying to themselves, *Why can't you do anything right?* or *You shouldn't have tried; you knew you couldn't do it,* or *See that—you're a failure!* But there is a huge difference between thinking *I have failed* and thinking *I am a failure.* Someone who has failed can learn from her mistakes and move on. It doesn't change who she is. But the person who tells himself, *I am a failure,* gives himself little hope of improvement. No matter what he does or where he goes, his failure stays with him because he has internalized it. He makes it an inseparable part of him. Asking someone who has convinced himself that he is a failure to be successful would be like asking an apple tree to produce cantaloupes. It can't be done.

How do you respond to failure?

□ *Assume that my failure shows that I'm a failure.*

□ *Understand that all successful people fail.*

If you're in the habit of assassinating your own character or questioning your talent every time something goes wrong, stop it. Making mistakes is like breathing; it's something you'll keep doing as long as you're alive. So learn to live with it and move on.

3. LET FAILURE REDIRECT YOU

Sometimes failure signals that it's time for a change in direction. If you keep hitting the wall, it may be time to back up and look for the door. If you keep taking the same detour, maybe it's not a detour but your main road. Still, when you experience failure after failure but your dream burns within you just as strongly as ever, keep going. Also recognize that some of the greatest accomplishments of life literally were birthed out of failure.

For example, look at the life of John James Audubon. He is considered a pioneer in wildlife study and preservation. But in the early 1800s, he was merely an unsuccessful shopkeeper in Louisville, Kentucky. He attempted to support himself and his wife, Lucy, in that occupation, but after struggling for eleven years, he finally went bankrupt. That failure prompted him to pursue his life's work—observing, drawing, and painting wildlife, the thing for which he will always be remembered.

If you're repeatedly experiencing failure but you want to fail forward, allow your mistakes to redirect you. Maybe you're working someplace where you don't really fit. That doesn't mean that you're bad or wrong. It just means that you need to make an adjustment. If one door repeatedly closes on you, don't stand there forever, wondering why you can't get it open. Look around for another open door. One may be standing open right now that you've continually overlooked.

Is it time to allow your repeated failure to redirect your course? If yes, why and how? _____

_____

4. KEEP A SENSE OF HUMOR

When all else fails, laugh. That's my motto. It's *easy* to laugh when everything is going great, but it's *important* to laugh when everything is going wrong. Nothing improves emotional health like laughter. It relieves stress and helps you quickly put your mistakes into perspective. Jerry Jenkins observed, "To err is human . . . but when you wear the eraser out ahead of the pencil, you're overdoing it." A prolific and successful writer, he understands the importance of a sense of humor when it comes to making mistakes.

As you make mistakes on the success journey, keep everything in a positive, humorous perspective. Try to look at life the way professional hockey coach Harry Neale did during a tough time. He quipped, "Last season, we couldn't win at home and we were losing on the road. My failure as a coach was that I couldn't think of anyplace else to play."

What humor can you find in a recent failure? _____

_____

5. ASK WHY, NOT WHO

When things go wrong, the natural tendency is to look for someone to blame. You can go all the way back to the Garden of Eden on this one. When God asked Adam what he had done, he said it was Eve's fault. Then when God questioned Eve, she blamed it on the snake. The same thing happens today. When you ask your daughter why she hit her brother, she says it's his fault. When the quarterback throws an interception, he says the receiver ran the wrong route. When you ask an employee why he didn't meet a deadline, he points his finger at someone else or cites circumstances beyond his control. And we won't even talk about all the lawsuits in which people blame others for their problems.

People who blame others for their failures never overcome them. They move from problem to problem, and as a result, they never experience success. To reach your potential, you must continually improve yourself, and you can't do that if you don't take responsibility for your actions and learn from your mistakes.

TAKE ACTION

The next time you experience a failure, think about why you failed instead of who was at fault. Try to look at it objectively so that you can do better next time. My friend Bobb Biehl suggests a list of questions to help you analyze any failure:

- What lessons have I learned? _____
  _____

- Am I grateful for this experience? _____
- How can I turn the failure into success? _____
  _____

- Practically speaking, where do I go from here? _____
  _____

- Who else has failed in this way before, and how can that person help me? _____
- How can my experience help others to keep from failing?
  _____

- Did I fail because of another person, because of my situation, or because of myself? _____
- Did I actually fail, or did I fall short of an unrealistically high standard?
  _____

- Where did I succeed as well as fail? _____
  _____

DAY 5

FAILING FORWARD

Yesterday we looked at the first five guidelines to help you change failure from detour to dividend. Today we will look at the remaining five.

TRANSFORMING FAILURE, CONTINUED

6. MAKE FAILURE A LEARNING EXPERIENCE

To be successful, you need to develop the ability to learn from your mistakes. You see, as Dr. Ronald Niednagel said, "Failure isn't failure unless you don't learn from it." That learning process changes what could be a permanent detour into a springboard to your potential.

Willingness to learn from failure and the ability to overcome it are inseparably linked to each other. If you're not continually learning, you're going to make the same mistakes over and over again. It's okay if you fall down as long as you learn something as you get up.

What is one thing you have learned or could learn from a recent failure?

_____

_____

_____

7. DON'T LET FAILURE KEEP YOU DOWN

Austin O'Malley asserted, "The fact that you have been knocked down is interesting, but the length of time you remain down is important." As you travel on the success journey, you will have problems. Are you going to give up and stay down, wallowing in your defeat, or are you going to get back on your feet as quickly as you can? As a college friend of mine used to say, "I'm never down; I'm either up or getting up."

A lot of people don't think that way. Some have been down so long that they're more comfortable lying down than they are getting back up. It has become a way of life for them. In fact, some not only stay down, they will also try to trip you up. Since they're no longer interested in getting up, their goal in life is to pull someone else down to make themselves feel better. *If you know people who act like this, steer clear of them.*

When you fall, make the best of it and get back on your feet. Learn what you can from your mistake, and then get back in the game. View your errors the way Henry Ford did his. He said, "Failure is the opportunity to begin again more intelligently."

8. USE FAILURE AS A GAUGE FOR GROWTH

When most people try to gauge success, they judge it according to how little failure they find. If they see flops or fumbles, they say, "He sure has messed up a lot. He's a failure." But that's exactly opposite of how successful people see failure. They already know what the editors of *Fortune* magazine found out several years ago when they analyzed successful people. Most successful people failed an average of *seven times* before they succeeded. You see, the more you try, the greater amount of failure you are likely to experience—and the greater amount of success. I don't know about you, but I'd rather reach 90 percent of my potential with plenty of mistakes than reach only 10 percent with a perfect score.

Each time you run the race and fail to finish first, examine your progress. Success is coming in fourth, exhausted but excited because you came in fifth the last time. It's making progress.

That's what it means to fail forward and avoid an unnecessary detour.

How are you making progress in spite of your failures?

_____

_____

9. See the Big Picture

Nothing is better at helping you deal with failure than perspective. Let me give you an example. Tom Landry, Chuck Noll, and Bill Walsh accounted for nine of the fifteen Super Bowl victories between 1974 and 1989. Do you know what else they have in common? They also had the worst first-season records of any head coaches in NFL history. Isn't that incredible? If they had judged their potential for success on their first year in professional football, they probably would have quit. If life were a snapshot and it had been taken during their losing seasons, they would have been in trouble. But life isn't a snapshot—it's a moving picture. They were able to overcome their failings and continue on the journey to reaching their potential.

Their failure was not final, and neither is yours. The next time you blow it, think about the big picture. There will be other days. We all make mistakes, but we can come back.

What is the big picture? Where and how does your recent failure fit into the time line of your life?

_____

_____

_____

10. Don't Give Up

I mentioned before that occasionally, failure is a sign that you should explore other opportunities. Although that is sometimes true, most often success comes as the result of good, old-fashioned tenacity. B. C. Forbes said, "History has demonstrated that the most notable winners usually encountered heartbreaking obstacles before they triumphed. They finally won because they refused to become discouraged by their defeats." Failure comes easily to everyone, but the price of success is perseverance.

The issue is not whether we're going to fail. Instead, when we fail, we need to determine whether we're going to fail backward or forward—that's the real question. The detours can make a person better or bitter. It's my choice. And it's also yours.

CHARTING THE COURSE

Turn to "My Road Map for Success" in the back of the workbook and complete Section B under *Growing to Reach My Maximum Potential.*

Week

7

ARE WE THERE YET?

PRINCIPAL QUESTIONS

DAY 1: What are the landmarks in my journey?

DAY 2: What will I have to give up in order to keep moving forward?

DAY 3: Am I willing to make the trade?

DAY 4: Do I see the big picture?

DAY 5: How can I continue to be persistent on the success journey?

DAY 1

IDENTIFYING LANDMARKS

On a flight to San Diego from the eastern United States, I was sitting in my seat trying to finish up a project I had been working on, and the pilot announced that we were starting to make our descent into the city. I could hear everyone around me straightening up seats and packing up belongings. But I kept working. I knew I had another few minutes before I needed to put my files back in my briefcase and get ready to leave the plane.

For many years I lived in San Diego, and whenever I flew there, I could always tell how close we were to landing. If I was sitting on the left side of the plane, when the Coronado Bridge came into view, spanning San Diego's beautiful bay, I knew we were only a few seconds from touching down on the runway at Lindbergh Field. That's when I packed up my stuff. You see, when you've taken a trip often, you come to know where you are and when you're about to reach your destination.

That ability seemed to be harder to develop when we were kids and taking trips by car. Do you remember that? Or if you have children of your own, you know what I'm talking about. The question they always seem to ask over and over again when you're driving a long distance in a car is this: "Are we there yet?" Sometimes they start asking it while you're still in the driveway.

Children certainly have a harder time knowing where they are on a trip than we adults do. Especially when they're young, they don't have a very good sense of the passage of time. And they don't naturally have a grasp of the big picture either. Let's face it: They don't have much experience traveling. They don't know what to expect, and they don't have the points of reference we do when it comes to travel.

Children can overcome their lack of perspective by learning the landmarks on the journey. For example, when I was a kid, I used to love it when our family packed up and drove from our home in Circleville, Ohio, to my grandparents' house in the suburbs of Detroit, Michigan. It took us quite a few hours to get there, and we didn't have to make the trip too many times before we began learning the landmarks. Our favorite was the city-limits sign of Finley, Ohio. We knew that when we got to Finley, we were at the halfway point, and the end of the trip finally seemed to be in sight.

LOOK FOR THE LANDMARKS

When it comes to the success journey, many adults are in the same boat as children. They seem continually to ask the question, *Am I there yet?* Part of that comes from an impatience about being successful, but it also indicates that too many people—despite their hard work—can't tell if they're making progress on the journey or not.

If you're silently asking yourself that question, the first thing I would tell you is to ask yourself a different question. You need to ask, *Am I headed there?* Remember, your goal is not to reach a destination; it's to take a journey. The second thing I would say is, *look for the landmarks.*

Whenever you're traveling and you're not quite sure where you are, you instinctively look for a landmark to get your bearings. I bet you could identify many places you've never even visited because you already know their landmarks. Take this simple quiz to find out.

Match the landmark with the place in which it's found:

Famous Landmarks	Cities*
1. Eiffel Tower	A. San Francisco, California
2. Super Dome	B. Rome, Italy
3. Coliseum	C. Walt Disney World, Florida
4. Big Ben	D. Washington, D.C.
5. Statue of Liberty	E. Jerusalem, Israel
6. Mount Fuji	F. Paris, France
7. Cinderella's Castle	G. London, England
8. Wailing Wall	H. Tokyo, Japan
9. Golden Gate Bridge	I. New York, New York
10. Lincoln Memorial	J. New Orleans, Louisiana

I imagine you got just about all of them right. In fact, you probably thought some of them were pretty easy. And you're right. Don't you wish the landmarks on your Road Map for Success were just as simple to identify? But think about what made this quiz so easy. You had already learned to associate those places with their landmarks, either because you've seen them yourself or because someone who has been there described them to you. Even if you have never been to Paris, you would recognize the Eiffel Tower when you saw it. The good news is that the same can be true of the landmarks on the success journey. All you need is someone who is acquainted with them to tell you what to look for, and you will recognize them.

You may be saying, "Why do I need to know about landmarks? Haven't I already identified my goals? Aren't they my landmarks?" These are good questions. But there are major differences between goals and landmarks. Goals generally provide an external target to shoot at in order to accomplish your dream. But success landmarks are internal, not external. They mark changes in you—in your thinking and attitudes—

*Answers: 1F, 2J, 3B, 4G, 5I, 6H, 7C, 8E, 9A, 10D

that are then reflected outwardly in how you act. The more landmarks you pass on the inside, the farther you will travel on the outside.

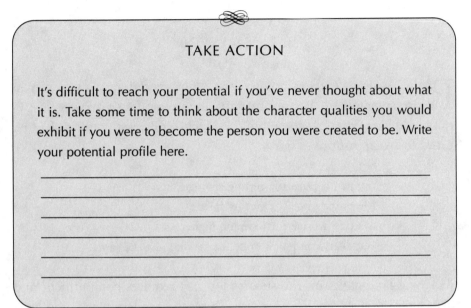

TAKE ACTION

It's difficult to reach your potential if you've never thought about what it is. Take some time to think about the character qualities you would exhibit if you were to become the person you were created to be. Write your potential profile here.

_____

_____

_____

_____

_____

_____

DAY 2

THE COST INVOLVED

Ralph Waldo Emerson pointed out, "For everything you gain, you lose something." Put another way, you could say that for everything you gain, you pay something. H. Jackson Brown, author of *Life's Little Instruction Book,* said,

> You pay a price for getting stronger.
> You pay a price for getting faster.
> You pay a price for jumping higher.
> [But also] you pay a price for staying just the same.

Reaching landmarks on the success journey requires commitment and persistence. It also requires sacrifice. To reach each landmark, you have to give up something of value. It's a series of trade-offs. Popular speaker and friend Ed Cole declared, "All of life is lived on levels and arrived at in stages."

Allow me to share several of the most significant trade-offs you will have to make in order to keep moving to a higher level during the success journey. To go to the highest level of success, you will need to choose . . .

ACHIEVEMENT OVER AFFIRMATION

When I was in my early twenties and working in my first job as a pastor, I was a people pleaser. Receiving affirmation from others was probably my predominant motivation in life. And when I didn't receive the recognition I desired, it really bothered me. I found out how much it bothered me when I attended my first general conference.

I was really excited about going to the conference because I had been very successful in my first position. I was anxious to share my accomplishments with everyone, including some of the guys I had gone to school with and other people I had gotten to know over the years.

I expected everyone I met to be happy for me. After all, we were all on the same team, working toward the same goal of helping people. But that was not what I found. Nobody wanted to hear about how well I was doing, and I didn't get the affirmation I wanted so much. I admit, I was probably a little too cocky at the time, and I may have rubbed a few people the wrong way. But I also learned an incredibly valuable lesson: *Affirmation from others is fickle and fleeting.* If you want to make an impact during your lifetime, you have to trade the praise you could receive from others for the things of value that you can accomplish. You can't be "one of the boys" and follow your destiny at the same time.

A friend once explained something to me that illustrates this concept very well. He grew up near the Atlantic Ocean, where people catch blue crabs for dinner. He told me that as they catch the crabs, they'll toss them into a bucket or basket. He said that if you have only one crab in the basket, you need a lid to keep it from crawling out, but if you've got two or more, you don't. That didn't make any sense to me until he explained further. He said that when there are several crabs, they will drag one another down so that none of them can get away.

I've found that some unsuccessful people act the same way. They do all kinds of things to keep others from getting ahead, trying to prevent them from improving themselves or their situation. They use all kinds of devices to keep others in the basket with them: playing politics, promoting mediocrity, role-playing, and so on. But the good news is that if people try to do that, you don't have to buy into their belief system. You can stay out of the basket by refusing to be a crab. You may have to face opposition and live through times of insecurity, but you'll also experience freedom, increased potential, and satisfaction. Raise yourself up, and raise others with you.

As aviator Charles Lindbergh put it, "Success is not measured by what a man accomplishes, but by the opposition he has encountered, and the courage with which he has maintained the struggle against overwhelming odds." Making the decision to trade affirmation for achievement may be one of the greatest obstacles you face. But when you're willing to do it, you have passed an important landmark on the success journey.

How can you choose achievement over affirmation? Do you need to change your focus? Who are the "crabs" that you need to stop listening to?

_____

_____

_____

EXCELLENCE OVER ACCEPTABILITY

Making a commitment to excellence is a fundamental step on the success journey. My friend Chuck Swindoll, chancellor of Dallas Theological Seminary, noted:

> Competitive excellence requires 100 percent all of the time. If you doubt that, try maintaining excellence by setting your standards at 92 percent. Or even 95 percent. People figure they're doing fine so long as they get somewhere near it. Excellence gets reduced to acceptable, and before long, acceptable doesn't seem worth the sweat if you can get by with adequate. After that, mediocrity is only a breath away.

I don't know about you, but I've never met a man or woman of success who hasn't passed the landmark of dedication to personal excellence. Believe it or not, lack of excellence has nothing to do with talent, personality, conditions, or luck. Excellence is always a choice. Willa A. Foster commented, "Quality is never an accident; it is always the result of high intention, sincere effort, intelligent direction and skillful execution; it represents the wise choice of many alternatives."

To achieve excellence over what's merely adequate, follow these recommendations:

- *Pay attention to details:* It takes a lot of little things to add up to 100 percent.

- *Seek continual improvement:* NBA coach Pat Riley said, "Excellence is the gradual result of always striving to do better."

- *Practice self-discipline:* Daily disciplines separate the excellent from the mediocre. If you want to change yourself, you must change something you do every day.

- *Maintain high personal standards:* D. Bruce Lockerbie, former scholar-in-residence at the Stony Brook School in New York, insisted, "Mediocrity isn't at root a national problem nor a corporate or institutional problem; nor a departmental problem. You see, mediocrity is first, a personal trait, a personal concession to less than our best. Mediocrity always begins with *me!*"

Your level of performance is a choice. You can settle for mediocrity, or you can strive for excellence. But know this: You can't make adequacy your goal and reach your potential.

How are you when it comes to . . .

Paying attention to details? _____

Seeking continual improvement? _____

Practicing self-discipline? _____

Maintaining high personal standards? _____

PERSONAL GROWTH OVER IMMEDIATE PLEASURE

We've already talked about personal growth in depth, but let me again remind you of its significance by communicating a statement by opera singer Beverly Sills: "There are no shortcuts to anyplace worth going."

You cannot dedicate yourself to pursuing pleasure and make genuine progress in your personal growth at the same time. You have to choose one or the other.

How did you contribute to your personal growth today?

_____

TAKE ACTION

Of the three trade-offs discussed today, which one will present the biggest obstacle on your success journey?

❑ Achievement over Affirmation

❑ Excellence over Acceptability

❑ Personal Growth over Immediate Pleasure

What choices will you need to make and what steps will you need to take in order to make this kind of trade-off in the future?

_____

_____

_____

DAY 3

MORE TRADE-OFFS

Yesterday we looked at what it would cost to reach a landmark: focusing on achievement, excellence, and personal growth. Today we continue to identify the trade-offs that will help you to move forward on the success journey. Choose . . .

FUTURE POTENTIAL OVER FINANCIAL GAIN

Many things in life have greater value than money. Possibly the greatest is personal potential. I've frequently traded financial gain for the prospect of future potential, particularly when managing my career. Aside from my role as the founder of INJOY, I've held only four positions in more than thirty years. When I accepted my first position straight out of college, I selected the lower paying of the two positions I was considering because it offered more opportunity for me to grow. And in the two and a half decades since then, I accepted only one position that offered a higher salary than the one I left. In every other case, I gladly accepted a cut in pay to receive the opportunity for greater potential.

Potential realized brings a person to a whole new level of living. Henry David Thoreau wrote, "If one advances confidently in the direction of his dreams, and endeavors to live the life which he has imagined, he will meet with a success unexpected in common hours. He will pass an invisible boundary; new, universal, and more liberal laws will begin to establish themselves around and within him; and he will live with the license of a higher order of beings."

Each time you relinquish the possibility of financial gain for an opportunity at future potential, you'll pass another major landmark on the success journey. Money often brings options, but it doesn't necessarily add value to your life. As you make decisions on the success journey, base them on potential, not dollars.

Under what circumstances would you take a lower-paying position?

_____

_____

_____

A NARROW FOCUS OVER SCATTERED INTERESTS

When you're young and first starting out, you would do well to try different things. That's one way for you to learn your strengths and discover your dreams. Besides, people with an I-don't-do-that-kind-of-work attitude who haven't paid their dues don't go very far. Being able to focus your attention almost exclusively on what you do best is a privilege you earn, not a right. But if you're going to go very far on the success journey, at some point you must narrow your focus. It's a major landmark you pass in the second half of your life.

If you've seen the movie *City Slickers,* you probably remember a scene between Billy Crystal, who played a city slicker out west on a vacation, and Jack Palance, who played a crusty old cowboy. Here's how their conversation went:

PALANCE: How old are you? Thirty-eight?

CRYSTAL: Thirty-nine.

PALANCE: Yeah. You all come out here about the same age. Same problems. Spend fifty weeks a year getting knots in your rope—then you think two weeks up here will untie them for you. None of you get it. *[Long pause]* Do you know what the secret of life is?

CRYSTAL: No, what?

PALANCE: It's this. *[Holds up his index finger]*

CRYSTAL: Your finger?

PALANCE: One thing. Just one thing. You stick to that and everything else
don't mean nothing.

CRYSTAL: That's great, but what's the one thing?

PALANCE: That's what you've got to figure out.

The cowboy was right. That's what you've got to figure out. And when you do, you then have to be willing to give up a lot of the less important things in your life for the opportunity to do that one big thing.

Look back at your dream or purpose statement from Week 2. Based on that statement, what is your one thing?

_____

_____

_____

SIGNIFICANCE OVER SECURITY

Most people enjoy feeling secure. It's a natural desire, one that psychologist Abraham Maslow recognized as important in the hierarchy of human needs. But to keep moving to a higher level and reach your potential, you also have to be willing to bypass another landmark and trade security for significance. Newsman Tom Brokaw observed, "It's easy to make a buck. It's a lot tougher to make a difference." And that's the essence of significance: the ability to make a difference in your world and the lives of others.

Bob Buford talks about the landmark ability of shifting your attention to significance in his book *Halftime*. As he sees it, our lives naturally break into two halves, with a midpoint usually falling somewhere between ages thirty and fifty. He says, "The first half of life has to do with getting and gaining, learning and earning . . . The second half is more risky because it has to do with living beyond the immediate." And he adds, "If you do not take responsibility for going into halftime and ordering your life so that your second half is better than the first, you will join the ranks of those who are coasting their way to retirement."[1] According to Buford, the key to making your second half count is to make the shift to significance. The result is that you will experience a life of purpose and see the fulfillment of your life's mission.

No matter when you make the change to significance, whether it's during your "halftime" or at some other time of life, know that it is one of the most significant, life-changing steps—and landmarks—on the success journey. It's a decision that's always worth the price.

How do you define significance?

_____

_____

TAKE ACTION

Of the three trade-offs discussed today, which one do you expect to face in the next few years?

❑ Future Potential over Financial Gain

❑ A Narrow Focus over Scattered Interests

❑ Significance over Security

What choices will you need to make and what steps will you need to take in order to prepare for this trade-off?

_____

_____

_____

DAY 4

THE SECRET TO CONTINUALLY TRADING UP

As you make progress on the success journey, you will frequently find yourself standing at a crossroads, and each time you do, you'll have to make a decision. Usually, you have three choices: gain something, lose something, or trade something.

Early in life, you make decisions that either add or subtract. But as time goes by, life gets more complicated, and if you want to keep going forward, you usually have to make more trade-offs. That's essential to recognize. Many unsuccessful people spend much of their lives standing at the crossroads, hoping for a situation where they can receive without giving anything up—but it rarely comes. As my friend David Jeremiah says, "You have to give up to go up." And the people who want to move forward without making any sacrifices get stuck at the crossroads and never go any farther on the success journey.

There are two keys to being able to make good trade-offs on the success journey. The first is the willingness to make sacrifices. The truth is that there is no success without sacrifice. If you are currently succeeding and you haven't made any sacrifices, then someone who has gone before you has made some that are benefiting you. And if you're making sacrifices now and you're not seeing any success, be assured, either you or someone else will enjoy the fruits of those sacrifices later on.

What sacrifices are you currently making for a better future?

_____

_____

_____

_____

When I was growing up, my parents taught me this concept. My dad always used to say, "John, you can pay now and play later, or you can play now and pay later. But either way, you're going to have to pay." Mom and Dad encouraged us to always pay first, and it became a lifestyle for me, my brother, Larry, and my sister, Trish. And along the way, I've also learned another truth: When you pay up front, you end up paying less, and you rarely find yourself running short on time or resources unexpectedly. Not only that, but when you pay first, the rewards are usually greater, and the number of your options increases.

The second secret to being able to make good trade-offs is old-fashioned persistence. You may have already heard this statement made by President Calvin Coolidge because McDonald's founder Ray Kroc was fond of quoting it: "Nothing in the world can take the place of persistence. Talent will not; nothing is more common than unsuccessful men with talent. Genius will not; unrewarded genius is almost a proverb. Education will not; the world is full of educated derelicts. Persistence and determination alone are omnipotent."

The good news is that you don't have to be born with persistence to have it. It's an attitude that you can develop and strengthen. If you're inclined to *give in* instead of *dig in,* increase your persistence level by doing the following.

STRATEGIES FOR GROWING PERSISTENCE

DEVELOP CHARACTER

No quality will ever serve you better on the success journey than character. Robert A. Cook declared, "There is no substitute for character. You can buy brains, but you cannot buy character." It not only helps you go far, but it helps you to make the right decisions along the way.

Take a look at the differences between the approaches to the success journey of people without character and with it:

Without Character	*With Character*
Does what's easiest	Does what's right
Controlled by moods	Controlled by values
Looks for excuses	Looks for solutions
Quits when challenged	Perseveres when challenged
Relies on external motivation	Relies on internal motivation
Words and actions don't match	Words and actions agree
Choices lead to failure	Choices add up to success

Olympic track champion Jesse Owens said:

> There is something that can happen to every athlete, every human being—it's the instinct to slack off, to give in to the pain, to give less than your best . . . the instinct to hope to win through luck or your opponents' not doing their best, instead of going to the limit and past your limit, where victory is always to be found. Defeating those negative instincts that are out to defeat us is the difference between winning and losing, and we face that battle every day of our lives.

Jesse Owens overcame those negative instincts. He set world records in *junior high school.* Then he continued to improve and set a world record in high school. When he got to college, he didn't let up. In one track meet he set three world records in less than an hour. And then in 1936, he showed the depth of his character and his dedication to persistence while competing in the Olympics in the heart of hostile Nazi Germany. He tied one world record and set three Olympic records while winning four Gold Medals. His accomplishments are a testimony to his dedication, and they are a solid example of the role of character when it comes to success.

How do you resemble the descriptions of a person with character? Are there any areas that you need to work on? Describe them.

_____

_____

_____

_____

FOCUS ON THE BIG PICTURE

Jesse Owens is certainly one of the most beloved champions in Olympic history, but not just winners show what it takes to be successful. On an October evening in 1968, a group of die-hard spectators remained in Mexico City's Olympic Stadium to see the last finishers of the Olympic marathon. More than an hour before, Mamo Wolde of Ethiopia had won the race to the exuberant cheers of onlookers. But as the crowd watched and waited for the last participants, it was getting cold and dark.

It looked as if the last runners were finished, so the remaining spectators were breaking up and leaving when they heard the sounds of sirens and police whistles coming from the marathon gate into the stadium. And as everyone watched, one last runner made his way onto the track for the last lap of the twenty-six-mile race. It was John Stephen Akhwari from Tanzania. As he ran the four-hundred-meter circuit, people could see that his leg was bandaged and bleeding. He had fallen and injured it during the race, but he hadn't let it stop him. The people in the stadium rose and applauded until he reached the finish line.

As he hobbled away, he was asked why he had not quit, injured as he was and having no chance of winning a medal. "My country did not send me to Mexico City to start the race," he answered. "They sent me to finish the race."[2]

Akhwari looked beyond the pain of the moment and kept his eye on the big picture of why he was there. As you make the success journey, keep in mind that your goal is to finish the race—to do the best you're capable of doing. You were created with a purpose. Make your decisions and plan your efforts accordingly.

When you look back at the journey you have taken up to this point, what are some landmarks that others might consider failures, but that you know contributed to your understanding of the bigger picture?

_____

_____

_____

GET RID OF EXCUSES

George Washington Carver said, "Ninety-nine percent of failures come from people who have the habit of making excuses." Carver was no stranger to adversity and could have easily made excuses for not succeeding. But that wasn't his way. Despite being born into slavery, he rose above his circumstances. He earned a master's degree in agriculture from Iowa State College, and he dedicated himself to teaching poor African American farmers. He developed an extension program at Alabama's Tuskegee Institute to take the classroom to the people in the South, teaching agriculture methods and home economics. And his research resulted in the development of hundreds of products made from crops such as peanuts and sweet potatoes. He did all that despite working with limited resources and opportunities because of segregation. Where others might have offered excuses, Carver achieved excellence.

Unsuccessful people can always find reasons for why they're not doing well. But successful people don't make excuses, even when they could justify them. No matter what the circumstances, they make the best of things and keep moving forward. That's what it means to persevere.

What is the most common excuse you hear from the people with whom you work? Do you find yourself making this same excuse? How do you avoid making this common excuse?

_____

_____

_____

UNDERSTAND THE ODDS

Once you understand what it takes to be successful, you understand the role that perseverance plays. You are able to beat the odds only if you have the discipline to keep going when others quit. As President Harry Truman said, "In reading the lives of great men, I found that the first victory they won was over themselves. Self-discipline with all of them came first."

I read the results of a survey conducted by the National Sales Executive Association. Here's what they found:

- 80 percent of all new sales are made after the fifth call to the same prospect.

- 48 percent of all salespersons make one call, then cross off the prospect.

- 25 percent quit after the second call.

- 12 percent call three times and then quit.

- 10 percent keep calling.

The people who make up that 10 percent of the sales force are the ones who make by far the majority of sales. And what's true for salespeople is also true for you. Whether you're an engineer, homemaker, educator, or entrepreneur, success doesn't result from superior talent, intellect, or luck. Persistance pays.

TAKE ACTION

E. M. Gray noted, "The successful person has the habit of doing the things that failures don't like to do. The successful person doesn't like doing them either, but his dislike is subordinated to the strength of his purpose." If you've allowed yourself to develop the habit of making excuses, make a commitment to change today. Trading excuses for excellence opens the door to many of the other positive trade-offs you'll need to make to be successful.

I will no longer make excuses about _____

Instead, I will become a more successful person by

_____

_____

DAY 5

STAYING HUNGRY

The author Rudyard Kipling wrote, "If you don't get what you want, it is a sign either that you did not seriously want it, or that you tried to bargain over the price." *How sincerely do you want to reach your potential and fulfill your purpose in life? Are you hungry for success?* It will take passion on your part to keep growing, learning, and trading up. And that passion will feed your persistence.

Over the years I've found that we have to make trade-offs throughout life in order to succeed, and only through wise exchanges can we reach our potential. The problem of many unsuccessful people is that they haven't worked to develop much worth trading. They want to trade being a couch potato to become the president of the New York Stock Exchange. But it doesn't work that way. You can make a trade only when you have something worth giving up. And when you do trade, you don't trade from the lowest level to the highest, skipping over all the levels in between. Usually, you're able to move only one level at a time—either up or down.

In 1995 I made the biggest trade of my life. I relinquished my position as the leader of Skyline Wesleyan Church in San Diego, California, the largest church in the denomination at the time. In church circles, it was a very prestigious position. I could easily have stayed there the rest of my life, giving pastoral care to the people and enjoying a lot of attention within the church community. But that would have meant turning my back on my purpose and giving up on developing my potential any further. So on July 9, 1995, I preached my last sermon at Skyline and traded a career I had poured my life into for twenty-six years for the ability to devote myself full-time to my company: The INJOY Group.

It was the right decision. One of my desires is to make a positive impact on the lives of more than ten million people during my lifetime by teaching and providing resources on leadership and personal growth. I don't know whether I will achieve it, but that doesn't matter. Success for me doesn't necessarily mean achieving that goal. It's taking the journey. More important is the fact that I made the trade-off to try to reach my potential. I passed another landmark on the success journey, and I know I'm heading in the right direction.

I hope you also set your sights on moving ever forward and upward on your journey. To do it, you'll need to make trade-offs along the way, often giving up something good in order to get something better. But it's a price worth paying. And as you make the trade-offs, keep looking for the landmarks. They will tell you how you're doing—and whether you're coming closer to reaching your potential.

CHARTING THE COURSE

Turn to "My Road Map for Success" in the back of the workbook and complete Section C under *Growing to Reach My Maximum Potential.*

Week

8

IS IT A FAMILY TRIP?

DAY 1
The People in My Family

DAY 2
Steps to Building a Strong Family

DAY 3
Spending Time and Dealing with Crisis *Together*

DAY 4
Constant Communication

DAY 5
Family Success = Personal Success

PRINCIPAL QUESTIONS

DAY 1: How does my family measure my success?

DAY 2: What steps am I taking to invest in my family?

DAY 3: How does my schedule reflect how important my family is to me?

DAY 4: What are some ways I can make communication easier in my family?

DAY 5: What is the most important relationship within my family?

DAY 1

THE PEOPLE IN MY FAMILY

Fairly early in our marriage, Margaret and I realized that in my career, I would often have the opportunity to travel. We decided that any time I got the chance to go someplace interesting or to attend an event that we both believed would be exciting, she would come along with me, even when it was difficult financially. We've done a pretty good job of following through on that commitment over the years. But because I travel so often and Margaret has frequently needed to stay home with our children, sometimes I've had to go on trips alone.

For example, I remember taking a trip about twenty years ago to Lancaster, Pennsylvania, to conduct a conference. Margaret and I love that area, especially the Amish country. The farms and old houses are absolutely beautiful. On that particular trip, I was fortunate enough to have a bit of free time to go exploring. So I drove around and enjoyed the countryside, had a delicious home-cooked meal at a little Pennsylvania Dutch restaurant, and did some shopping.

While I was in the area, I decided that I wasn't going home without a handmade quilt for Margaret. I asked around to find the best place to buy one, and I ended up at a farmhouse in the country that had more than a dozen quilts hanging on the front porch. I bought her the most beautiful one they had and had them wrap it up. I couldn't wait to give it to her when I got home. And as I hoped, when she opened the package, she was delighted.

I've really enjoyed bringing gifts back to Margaret and the kids over the years. And it's fun to tell them about some of the things that happened. It's a way to share the trip with them. But I've discovered that no matter what you bring back or what you do to include your family after you've returned from the trip, it doesn't compare to having them there with you.

I love taking my family with me—including on business trips—because I get the chance to share the opportunities and the rewards of the journey. Together Margaret, Elizabeth, Joel Porter, and I have been to the capitals of Europe, the jungles of South America, the teeming cities of Korea, the rugged outback of Australia, and on safari in South Africa. We've met wonderful people of every race and a multitude of nationalities. We've had the chance to see and do things that will remain in our memories for the rest of our lives.

Those trips have been fun. But our travels around the globe don't in any way compare to another trip I've taken them on: the success journey. What would it profit me to gain the whole world and lose my family?

As I talk to people about the idea of the success journey and listen to them talk about their experiences, I hear interesting stories. For example, Stephanie Wetzel told me about an incident from a choir trip she took in high school. She and a choir of about fifty were traveling together across country on a bus along with her choir director and his whole family: his wife, high-school-age daughter, and seven-year-old son.

The worst part of the trip was the long, hot drive across Texas. To break up the monotony, they would pull over at a rest stop every now and then to give the kids a chance to stretch their legs and go to the bathroom. After they had made one of these stops out in the middle of nowhere, they had been driving for almost an hour when they made a discovery. They couldn't find the director's son.

They immediately turned around and headed back toward the rest area. The director kept pleading with the driver to go faster. They couldn't stop thinking about some of the terrible things that could have happened to him in an hour's time. By the time they finally arrived at the rest stop, they were in a panic. Everyone scrambled out of the bus and began looking for him. It didn't take long. One of the boys found him in the men's room—killing flies. He hadn't even realized he had been missed.

If you have children, you know how traumatic an incident like that can be for a parent. Yet as much as parents love their children, every day many of them walk away from their families in the pursuit of success.

It's almost as though they're driving down the road and they get pretty far along before they realize they've left members of their family behind. The tragedy is that many value their careers, success, or personal happiness more than they do their families. They decide that it's too much work to go back, so they just keep driving. They leave their spouses and children behind to fend for themselves, just like that little boy would have had to if the choir director hadn't gone back for him.

Did you know that according to the Bureau of Labor Statistics, families dissolve at a greater rate in the United States than in any other major industrialized country? And we also lead in the number of fathers absent from the home. U.S. divorce laws are the most permissible in the world, and people are using them at an alarming rate.[1] To some people, marriages and families have become acceptable casualties in the pursuit of success.

But many people are now realizing that the hope of happiness at the expense of breaking up a family is an illusion. You can't give up your marriage or neglect your children and gain true success. Building and maintaining strong families benefit us in every way, including helping us make the success journey. Nick Stinnet asserted more than a decade ago, "When you have a strong family life, you receive the message that you are loved, cared for, and important. The positive intake of love, affection, and respect . . . gives you inner resources to deal with life more successfully."

I believe my greatest accomplishment in life was getting Margaret to marry me. We're partners in everything, and I know that I wouldn't have experienced any measure of success in life without her. But my gratitude to her and the children doesn't come from what they've brought me. It comes from who they are to me. You see, several years ago I realized that all the success in the world means nothing if you aren't loved and respected by those closest to you. When I reach the end of my days, I don't want Margaret, Elizabeth, or Joel Porter to say that I was a good author, speaker, pastor, or leader. My desire is that the kids think I was a good father and that Margaret thinks I was a good husband. That's what matters most. It's the measure of true success.

TAKE ACTION

Whether you are married or single, young or old, think about the people whom you consider to be family. You may have a unique situation where your "family" is made up of people who are not related to you, but who have played a special part in your life over the years. Whatever the case may be, list the names of those people below, and beside each name write out a phrase indicating how each would measure your relationship with them.

NAME   THEIR MEASURE OF YOUR SUCCESS

_____   _____

_____   _____

_____   _____

_____   _____

_____   _____

STEPS TO BUILDING A STRONG FAMILY

Good marriages and strong families are joys, and they make the success journey worthwhile. But they don't just happen on their own. Dr. R. C. Adams, who studied thousands of marriages over a ten-year period, found that only 17 percent of the unions he observed could be considered truly happy. And Jarle Brors, director of the Institute of Marriage and Family Relations in Washington, D.C., said, "We are finally realizing that we have to go back to the basics in order to reestablish the type of families that give us the type of security that children can grow up in." If we want to have solid families and healthy marriages, we have to work hard to create them.

For the rest of the week we will be concentrating on ways to build stronger families. Today we will start with one of the most important and fundamental guidelines: appreciation.

EXPRESSING APPRECIATION FOR EACH OTHER

I once heard someone joke that home is the place where family members go when they are tired of being nice to other people. Unfortunately, some homes seem to work that way. A salesman spends his day treating his clients with the utmost kindness, often in the face of rejection, in order to build his business, but he is rude to his wife when he comes home. Or a doctor spends the day being caring and compassionate with her patients, but she comes home exhausted and blows up at her children.

How do you treat your family compared to the way you treat others?

_____

_____

_____

To build a strong family, you have to make your home a supportive environment. Psychologist William James observed, "In every person from the cradle to the grave, there is a deep craving to be appreciated." Feeling appreciated brings out the best in people. And when that appreciation comes in the home and is coupled with acceptance, love, and encouragement, the bonds between family members grow, and the home becomes a safe haven for everyone.

I believe that the ability to appreciate each other comes first from the ability to understand how your family members are designed. If you're married, you're probably already aware of many of the differences between you and your spouse. You probably even expect differences. But you may be surprised to know that your children are also likely to be different—not only from each other but from you and your spouse.

A book written by Florence Littauer called *Personality Plus* helped Margaret and me understand our differences with the kids and each other. The information came as a great surprise and relief. It gave us insight into the four basic personality types:

- *Sanguine:* desires fun; is outgoing, relationship oriented, witty, easygoing, popular, artistic, emotional, outspoken, and optimistic.

- *Melancholy:* desires perfection; is introverted, task oriented, artistic, emotional, goal oriented, organized, and pessimistic.

- *Phlegmatic:* desires peace; is introverted, unemotional, strong willed, relationship oriented, pessimistic, and purpose driven.

- *Choleric:* desires power or control; is strong willed, decisive, goal oriented, organized, unemotional, outgoing, outspoken, and optimistic.[2]

Everyone in your family—and for that matter, every person you meet—will exhibit characteristics primarily from one or two of these personality types.

For each person in your family, list the personality type that best describes him or her (sanguine, melancholy, phlegmatic, or choleric).

Family Member	Personality Type
_____	_____
_____	_____
_____	_____
_____	_____
_____	

Another tool for helping you appreciate each family member's uniqueness is the ability to see each other's natural talents or "intelligences" as described by Thomas Armstrong in his book 7 *Kinds of Smart*. When most of us look at others, we tend to measure them against our own talents or against a traditional academic view of intelligence. But Armstrong describes seven different kinds of intelligence that all people have to one degree or another:

1. Linguistic Intelligence (the ability to use words): People who are smart in this area can argue, persuade, entertain, or instruct effectively using the spoken word. They often love puns, word games, and trivia, they read voraciously and write clearly. Examples: William Shakespeare, James Joyce, and Abraham Lincoln.

2. Logical-Mathematical Intelligence (working with numbers and logic): People with talent in this area have the ability to reason, create hypotheses, think in terms of cause and effect, and find conceptual or numerical patterns in the things around them. Examples: Albert Einstein, Sir Isaac Newton, and Bill Gates.

3. Spatial Intelligence (thinking in pictures and images): People with spatial ability can perceive, transform, and re-create different aspects of the visual spatial world. They are sensitive to visual details, can visualize vividly, orient themselves in three-dimensional space, and often draw or sketch ideas. Examples: Pablo Picasso, Thomas Edison, and Frank Lloyd Wright.

4. *Musical Intelligence* (perceiving, appreciating, and producing rhythms and melodies): People with this intelligence have a good ear, can keep time, sing in tune, and listen to music with discernment. Examples: Johann Sebastian Bach, George Gershwin, and Beverly Sills.

5. *Bodily-Kinesthetic Intelligence* (knowing the physical self): People with gifts in this area are good at controlling their body movements, handling objects skillfully, and performing other physical activities. Examples: Michael Jordan, Charlie Chaplin, and Fred Astaire.

6. *Interpersonal Intelligence* (understanding and working with people): Those who have this intelligence are able to perceive and be responsive to the moods, temperaments, intentions, and desires of others. Examples: Ronald Reagan, Mother Teresa, and Zig Ziglar.

7. *Intrapersonal Intelligence* (knowing the inner self): People gifted in this area are introspective, good at assessing their own feelings, and capable of deep spiritual or intellectual thought. Examples: John Wesley, Laurence Olivier, and Joyce Brothers.[3]

For each person in your family, list the top two or three intelligence types that best describes him or her.

Family Member	Intelligence Type
_____	_____
_____	_____
_____	_____
_____	_____
_____	_____

All of us have a blend of strengths and weaknesses in each area that makes us unique. And once you have a good understanding of how the other members of your family are designed, it becomes easier for you to be more sensitive to and express love for them.

I've heard that for every negative remark to a family member, it takes four positive statements to counteract the damage. That's why it's so important to focus on the positive aspects of each other's personality and to express unconditional love, both verbally and nonverbally. Then the home becomes a positive environment for everyone.

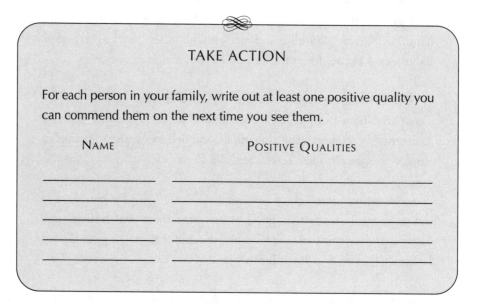

TAKE ACTION

For each person in your family, write out at least one positive quality you can commend them on the next time you see them.

NAME   POSITIVE QUALITIES

_____   _____

_____   _____

_____   _____

_____   _____

_____   _____

DAY 3

Spending Time and Dealing with Crisis *Together*

It's been said that the American home has become a domestic cloverleaf upon which family members pass each other while en route to a multitude of places and activities. That seems to be true. When I was a kid, I spent a lot of time with my parents, brother, and sister. We went on family vacations, usually in the car. We had regular Saturday outings where we did things together such as swimming, watching a ball game, or going to the movies. And we ate dinner together every day. That was our special family time, and we knew not to make any plans that conflicted with it.

As a parent, I've found it hard to keep that tradition alive. We've been good about planning and taking vacations, but sometimes we've had to be creative to have everyday time together. For example, when the children were younger, I always tried to drive them to school in the morning. And I made it a practice to spend a few minutes with them individually at bedtime. But with all the things going on in our busy lives, we found that the only way to get time together was to plan it carefully.

STRUCTURE YOUR LIVES TO SPEND TIME TOGETHER

Every month, I spend several hours examining my traveling schedule, figuring out what lessons I need to write, thinking about the projects I have to complete, and so on. And at that time, I'll plan my work for the whole month. But before I mark any dates for work, I write in all the important dates for family activities. I'll block out time for birthdays, anniversaries, ball games, theater performances, graduation ceremonies, concerts, and romantic dinners. I'll schedule special one-on-one time with Margaret and each of the kids so that we can continue to build our relationships. Once those are set, I'll plan my work schedule around them. I've done this for years, and it's been the only thing that's prevented my work from squeezing my family out of the schedule. I've found that if I don't strategically structure my life to spend time with my family, it won't happen.

Look at your calendar. How much time have you planned to spend with your family? Are there ways to find additional time to spend with them?

_____

_____

_____

Besides scheduling special events, it's also important to observe family traditions or just have fun. Both create special memories and bondedness among family members. And traditions have the added value of creating continuity within the family, even amid times of rapid change. It doesn't really matter what you do as long as you enjoy it together: watching fireworks on the Fourth of July, trimming the Christmas tree, having a Passover Seder, going to Disneyland when school gets out, cooking and eating special foods at Thanksgiving. Be creative and start your own traditions.

What special traditions do you have with your family? What new tradition could you start this year?

_____

_____

_____

DEAL WITH CRISIS IN A POSITIVE WAY

Every family experiences problems, but not all families respond to them in the same way. And that often separates a family that's close from one that's barely holding together. I've noticed that some people pursuing success seem to avoid the home environment. I suspect that one reason is that they are not able to handle family crisis situations well. They find it easier to try to avoid the problems altogether. But that's not a solution.

How do you respond to crisis in relation to your family?

❑ *I keep problems to myself. There's no reason to drag my family into it.*

❑ *I share problems with my family only when I have to. I would rather avoid the situation.*

❑ *I share my problems with my family so they will have a better understanding of what is going on.*

M. Scott Peck, author of *The Road Less Traveled, has* offered some remarkable insights on the subject of problems and how we handle them:

> It is in this whole process of meeting and solving problems that life has meaning. Problems are the cutting edge that distinguishes between success and failure. Problems call forth our courage and wisdom; indeed they create our courage and our wisdom. It is only because of problems that we grow mentally and spiritually . . . It is through the pain of confronting and resolving problems that we learn. As Benjamin Franklin said, "Those things that hurt, instruct."

If we are to grow as families and be successful at home as well as in the other areas of our lives, we must learn to cope with the difficulties we find there. Here are some strategies to help you with the problem-solving process.

ATTACK THE PROBLEM, NEVER THE PERSON

Always try to be supportive of each other. Remember, you're all on the same side. So don't take your frustrations out on people. Instead, attack the problem.

GET ALL THE FACTS

Nothing can cause more damage than jumping to false conclusions during a crisis. Before you try to find solutions, be sure you know what's really going on.

LIST ALL THE OPTIONS

This may sound a bit analytical, but it really helps because you can look at emotional subjects with some objectivity. Besides, if you had a problem at work, you would probably be willing to go through this process. Give any family problem at least as much time and energy as you would a professional one.

CHOOSE THE BEST SOLUTION

As you decide on a solution, always remember that people are your priority. Make your choices accordingly.

LOOK FOR THE POSITIVES IN THE PROBLEM

As Dr. Peck said, the tough things give us a chance to grow. No matter how bad things look at the moment, just about everything has something positive that comes from it.

NEVER WITHHOLD LOVE

No matter how bad things get or how angry you are, never withhold your love from your spouse or children. Sure, tell them how you feel. Acknowledge the problems. But continue loving family members unconditionally through it all.

This last point is the most important of all. When you feel loved and supported by your family, you can weather nearly any crisis. And you can truly enjoy success.

TAKE ACTION

What problem is your family currently facing? Look at the strategy list and work your way through the problem by using this list as a guideline.

_____

_____

How can we attack the problem, not a person?

_____

_____

Do we have all the facts? What else do we need to know?

_____

_____

What are our options?

_____

_____

What is the best solution? (Discuss this with family members.)

_____

_____

What positive things could come from this problem?

_____

_____

How can we reassure one another of our love while we deal with this problem?

_____

_____

DAY 4

CONSTANT COMMUNICATION

An article in the *Dallas Morning News* reported that the average couple married ten years or more spends only thirty-seven minutes a week in meaningful communication. I could hardly believe it. Compare that to the fact that the average American spends almost five times longer than that watching television every day! No wonder so many marriages are in trouble.

> *How much time do you spend each week in meaningful communication with your family?*

❑ *Less than thirty minutes*

❑ *Between thirty minutes and an hour*

❑ *Between one hour and three hours*

❑ *More than five hours*

Just like anything else, good communication doesn't happen by itself. It must be developed, and that process takes time and effort. Here are some suggestions for helping you do exactly that.

STRATEGIES FOR IMPROVING COMMUNICATION

DEVELOP PLATFORMS FOR COMMUNICATION

Be creative about finding reasons to talk to each other. Take walks together as a family where you can talk. Call your spouse a couple of times during the day. Meet for lunch one day a week. Offer to drive the kids to soccer practice so you can talk. Communication can happen almost anywhere.

CONTROL COMMUNICATION KILLERS

The television and the telephone probably steal the most family communication time. Restrict the amount of time you give to these activities, and you'll be amazed by how much time you have to talk.

ENCOURAGE HONESTY AND TRANSPARENCY IN CONVERSATIONS

Differences of opinion are healthy and normal in a family. Encourage all family members to speak their minds, and when they do, never criticize or ridicule them.

ADOPT A POSITIVE COMMUNICATION STYLE

Be conscious of the way you interact with your family members. You may have adopted a style that stifles open communication. Take a look at the following table.

COMMUNICATION STYLES

COMMUNICATION STYLE	RESULTS OF THE COMMUNICATION PROCESS	DIRECTION IT TAKES PEOPLE	EFFECT ON RECIPIENT
Retaliation	Destroys Positive Communication	Against Each Other	Degrading
Domination	Destroys Open Communication	Over Each Other	Intimidating
Isolation	Destroys Hope of Communication	Away from Each Other	Frustrating
Cooperation	Develops Positive, Open Communication	With Each Other	Encouraging

*What is your natural communication style?*_____

If you're in the habit of using any communication style other than the cooperative one, begin working immediately to change. If you normally retaliate, turn the other cheek. If you dominate, let others speak first and seek to meet their needs. If you usually isolate yourself, force yourself to interact with others—even when you don't feel like it. You'll have to do these things if you want to build a better relationship with your family.

SHARE THE SAME VALUES

I read an article by Dottie Enrico in *USA Today* called "Survey: Fallen Heroes Among 'Most Admired' Athletes." It came out during O. J. Simpson's criminal trial for murder. The article reported on a survey performed by Sponsorship Research International of Stamford, Connecticut, and the results were astounding. Among the top twenty athletes listed as most admired were Mike Tyson, O. J. Simpson, and Tonya Harding. The article went on to say, "Behavioral specialists say the presence of Tyson (a convicted rapist), Simpson (on trial for murder), and Harding (who pleaded guilty to conspiracy) on the list is a disturbing statement about American values."

One of the reasons people seem to be going astray when it comes to values is that families don't give them the attention they once did. Boston College Education Professor William Kilpatrick said:

> There is a myth that parents don't have the right to instill their values in their children. Once again, the standard dogma here is that children must create their own values. But of course, children have precious little chance to do that . . . Does it make sense for parents to remain neutral bystanders when everyone else from script writers, to enter-

tainers, to advertisers, to sex educators insist on selling their values to children?[4]

If you have children, who are the predominant people influencing their choices and values right now?

_____

_____

_____

Common values strengthen a family and are especially beneficial to children as they grow up. A study conducted by the Search Institute showed that in single-parent homes, children whose parent expresses and enforces standards thrive at twice the rate of children who don't have values promoted in a similar way. And that doesn't even take into account whether the values are what we would consider positive.

The best way to get started in working toward sharing common values in your family is to identify the values you want to instill. If you're like most families, you've never done that before. But to be able to live them out, you first have to find them out. They are the three to seven things you're willing to go to the mat for.

Let me list for you the five we've identified in the Maxwell family so that you have an idea of what I'm talking about:

1. Commitment to God
2. Commitment to personal and family growth
3. Commonly shared experiences
4. Confidence in ourselves and others
5. The desire to make a contribution in life

The values you choose might be different from ours, but you need to identify them. No target makes for sloppy aim.

TAKE ACTION

You need to identify the values that are specific to your family. If you've never done it before, set aside some time to talk about your values with your spouse and children. If your kids are older, include them in the process of identifying the values. Make it a discussion time. And never be reluctant to take on the role of model and teacher of your family's values. If you don't do it, someone else will.

As a family, our values are:

1. _____
_____

2. _____
_____

3. _____
_____

4. _____
_____

5. _____
_____

DAY 5

FAMILY SUCCESS = PERSONAL SUCCESS

NBA coach Pat Riley said, "Sustain a family life for a long period of time and you can sustain success for a long period of time. First things first. If your life is in order you can do whatever you want." There is definitely a correlation between family success and personal success. Not only does building a strong family lay the groundwork for future success, but it also gives life deeper meaning.

I believe that few people have ever been truly successful without a positive, supportive family. No matter how great people's accomplishments are, I think they're still missing something when they're working without the benefit of those close relationships. True, some people are called to be single, but they are rare. For most people, a good family helps you know your purpose and develop your potential, and it helps you enjoy the journey along the way with an intensity that isn't possible otherwise. And when it comes to sowing seeds that benefit others, who could possibly derive greater benefit from you than your own family members?

BUILD YOUR MARRIAGE

If you are married, the best thing you can do to strengthen your family is to build your marriage relationship. It's certainly the best thing you can do for your spouse, but it also has an incredibly positive impact on your children. My friend Josh McDowell wisely stated, "The greatest thing a father can do for his children is to love their mother." And the greatest thing a mother can do for her children is to love their father.

A common missing ingredient in many marriages is the dedication to make things work. Marriages may start because of love, but they finish because of commitment. Sexuality researcher Dr. Alfred Kinsey, who studied six thousand marriages and three thousand divorces, revealed: "There may be nothing more important in a marriage than a determination that it shall persist. With such a determination, individuals force themselves to adjust and to accept situations which would seem sufficient grounds for a breakup, if continuation of the marriage were not the prime objective." If you want to help your spouse, your children, and yourself, then become committed to building and sustaining a strong marriage.

In what ways do you show that you are committed to your marriage?

_____

_____

_____

Sometimes we need a jolt to wake us up to the less-than-acceptable way we've been interacting with the people in our families. I know that happened to a friend of mine whom I met through my involvement with the Christian men's movement, PromiseKeepers. He said that one day when his daughter was in first or second grade, she and her classmates were asked to draw a picture of their families. She loved to draw, so she willingly tackled the assignment. That evening, she proudly brought her artwork home and showed it to her parents. When my friend looked at the picture, he said, "What's this a picture of?"

"That's us and our house," she answered. "The teacher asked us to draw a picture of our family."

He looked at the picture more carefully and saw that everyone was there—except him. "Sweetheart," he asked, "is Daddy in the picture?"

"No," she said.

"Why not?"

"This is a picture of us at home, and you're never here," she explained.

It was as if she had dropped a piano on him. She had said it as a simple fact, without malice or any desire to inflict guilt. That was the day he decided that he was going to turn the bus around and come back for his family.

If you've been traveling down the road on the success journey but you've neglected to bring your family along, it's time for you to make a U-turn. Go back and pick up the people who matter most in your life. And commit yourself to following a road map that includes them. What greater joy could there be than a family trip of success?

CHARTING THE COURSE

Turn to "My Road Map for Success" in the back of the workbook and complete Section A under *Sowing Seeds That Benefit Others.*

Week

9

WHO ELSE SHOULD I TAKE WITH ME?

DAY 1
Living at the Highest Level

DAY 2
Finding the Right People for the Journey

DAY 3
Leadership Potential

DAY 4
Someone to Count On

DAY 5
Choosing the Team

PRINCIPAL QUESTIONS

DAY 1: How are the people closest to me affecting my success journey?

DAY 2: How can I identify the people I want to recruit for my success journey?

DAY 3: Do I possess the leadership qualities that I am looking for in others?

DAY 4: Whom do I trust and turn to?

DAY 5: Whom am I going to take with me on the success journey?

DAY 1

LIVING AT THE HIGHEST LEVEL

When our daughter Elizabeth was in her senior year of high school, Margaret and I decided to take her (and the rest of the family) on a trip to Hawaii as a graduation present. We told her about our plan several months in advance because Elizabeth isn't crazy about surprises. She likes to have time to process decisions and prepare herself mentally for change. We also told her that she could invite one of her girlfriends to go along with her on the trip.

For three months Elizabeth agonized over whom she should take with her. She had many friends to choose from and didn't want to hurt anyone's feelings. But she knew that no matter how she handled it or which girl she picked, a couple of her closest friends might feel hurt and left out.

A couple of times Margaret and I got impatient and wanted to make the decision for her. That just reflects our personalities. But we resisted the temptation. We understood that no one can choose someone else's traveling companion. And Elizabeth finally made her choice, picking the girl she thought would be most compatible with her. The result: both had a wonderful time.

Maybe you haven't thought about it, but you're going to have to make similar decisions as you take the success journey. One of the questions you will need to ask yourself is, *Whom should I take along with me?* Certainly if you have a family, you will take them with you. But who else should go along? You might be thinking, *Why would I want to take anybody else? If I can make the journey myself and even take my family with me, I don't need anyone else, do I?* Although you may be able to take the journey without others, I can tell you that you will never be able to reach your maximum potential and go to the highest level if you take the journey alone.

Over time I've learned this meaningful lesson: *The people closest to me determine my level of success or failure.* The better they are, the better I am. And if I want to go to the highest level, I can do it only with the help of other people. We have to take each other higher.

I discovered this truth about fifteen years ago as I approached my fortieth birthday. At that time I already felt very successful. I was the leader of the largest church in my denomination. I had published five books. I was recognized as an authority on leadership, and I was teaching the subject in conferences and via taped lessons every month. I was fulfilling the purpose for which I was created, daily growing to my potential, and sowing seeds that benefited others. But my desire was to make an even greater impact on others. I wanted to go to a whole new level.

My problem was that I had hit a wall. I was running a large organization that required much of my time. I had a family. I was writing books, leadership lessons, and sermons continually. And on top of that, my travel schedule was packed. I couldn't squeeze another thing into my schedule. That's when I made the amazing discovery. The only places where my influence and productivity were growing were where I had identified potential leaders and developed them.

My intention in developing leaders had been to help them improve themselves, but I found I was benefiting too. Spending time with them had been like investing money. They had grown, and at the same time I had reaped incredible dividends. That's when I realized that if I was to make it to the next level, I was going to have to extend myself through others. I would find leaders and pour my life into them, doing my best to bring them up to a new level. And as they improved, so would I.

THE PEOPLE AROUND YOU DETERMINE YOUR SUCCESS

That process has changed my life. I've gone farther on the success journey and to a higher level than I ever dreamed about. And the people around me deserve a huge amount of the credit for my success. I am able to do more things, teach more seminars, write more books, and touch many more lives, thanks to them. There is almost no limit to what I can accomplish because of the wonderful people I have on my team.

TAKE ACTION

Write down the names of the people whom you might choose to take on your journey. Try to think of at least seven.

1. _____
2. _____
3. _____
4. _____
5. _____
6. _____
7. _____

DAY 2

FINDING THE RIGHT PEOPLE FOR THE JOURNEY

Having exceptional people on the journey with you doesn't happen by accident. It's true that the greater your dream, the greater the people who will be attracted to you. But that alone isn't enough. You need to know what to look for in order to find the best possible people. And you need to start by making sure they're compatible with you, just as Elizabeth did with her friend before going to Hawaii.

Even before you begin looking at the qualities that make a person right for going on the journey with you, you need to ask yourself a few questions about each person. The first one is, *Does this person want to go?* That was a hard lesson for me to learn because early on, I wanted to take everybody with me. I'm a fun-loving, sanguine kind of guy, and I want to be successful. I just assumed that everyone wanted what I did—to be successful and to strive to reach his potential. But that's not true. Many people have no desire to grow whatsoever. Their goal is to find a comfortable place so that they can go on cruise control for the rest of their lives.

And a person may not want to go on the journey with you for other reasons. For example, he may want to grow just as much as you do but his interests don't coincide with yours. As a result, there is no compatibility. Margaret really helped me learn this lesson, and now I try to recruit only the people who are interested in going with me.

The second question you need to ask is, *Is this person able to go?* There has to be a match between the journey you want to take and the person's gifts and talents. For example, let's say your dream is to be a professional country singer. And you want to make a good living so that you can help inner-city kids. The people you'll want to join you on the journey will probably have musical talent, business skills, or experience ministering to inner-city kids. Anyone not having talents in these areas is much less likely to be compatible with you and your dream.

The third question you should ask is, *Can this person make the trip without me?* You can look at some people and know they have everything it takes to make the success journey on their own. They have their own road map and are not going to need your help. In fact, they are likely to be in a position to take others on the journey with them, just as you are going to do. In that case, make friends with them and try to keep in touch. Though you may not take the journey together, you may be able to help one another down the road as colleagues.

For each of the people you listed yesterday, answer yes or no to each question:

Name	Does this person want to go?	Is this person able to go?	Can this person make the trip without me?

Once you've settled these issues, you're ready to look for people whom you will be able to help reach their potential and who will also help you reach yours. And that means finding potential leaders. Everything rises and falls on leadership.

Over the years, I've narrowed down what I look for in a potential leader to only ten things, and I want to share them with you. For the next three days we will look at each quality. Today, we start with the two most important ones.

PEOPLE TO TAKE ON THE TRIP

1. PEOPLE WHO MAKE THINGS HAPPEN

Millionaire philanthropist Andrew Carnegie said, "As I grow older, I pay less attention to what men say. I just watch what they do." I've found that to be sound advice. As I've watched what people do, I've discovered that the ones I want with me are people who make things happen. These people discover resources in places you thought were barren. They find prospects where you believed there weren't any. They create opportunities where you thought none existed. They take something average and make it exceptional. They never make excuses—they always find a way to make things happen.

Even under the worst of circumstances—or with major disabilities—people with potential make things happen. Dr. George W. Crane observed, "There is no future in any job. The future lies in the person who holds the job." If you want to go far on the success journey, partner with others who know how to make things happen.

List the names of a few people you know who make things happen.

_____   _____

_____   _____

_____   _____

2. PEOPLE WHO SEE AND SEIZE OPPORTUNITIES

Many people are able to recognize an opportunity after it has already passed them by. But seeing opportunities coming—that's a different matter. Opportunities are seldom labeled. That's why you have to learn what they look like and how to seize them.

The best people to take with you on the journey don't sit

back and wait for opportunities to come to them. They make it their responsibility to go out and find them. It's similar to the two ways you can go about picking up someone you don't know from the airport. One way is to make a sign with the name of the person you're expecting, stand near the baggage-claim area, hold up the sign, and wait for the person to find you. If he sees you, great. If he doesn't, you keep waiting. The other way is to find out what the person looks like, position yourself strategically near the right gate, and search for him until you find him. There is a world of difference between the two approaches.

Ellen Metcalf said, "I would like to amend the idea of being in the right place at the right time. There are many people who were in the right place but didn't know it. You have to recognize when the right place and the right time fuse and take advantage of that opportunity. There are plenty of opportunities out there. You can't sit back and wait." Good potential leaders know that, and they don't rely on luck either. According to Walter P. Chrysler, founder of the automotive corporation that bears his name, "The reason so many people never get anywhere in life is because when opportunity knocks, they are out in the backyard looking for four-leaf clovers."

Of the people around you, who always seems able to recognize opportunities and grab hold of them? List their names below.

_____   _____
_____   _____
_____   _____

TAKE ACTION

What event or invention do you consider to be one of the greatest accomplishments of the twentieth century?

_____

Who were some of the people involved in this accomplishment? (You may need to do a little research.)

_____   _____

_____   _____

_____   _____

_____   _____

Was the accomplishment the result of one person's dream? _____

Too often we focus on solo achievement, when actually no lone individual has ever done anything of significant value. Every great dreamer who has seen his dream actualized has worked with others. To live at the highest level and have significant success, we must include people on our success journey.

DAY 3

LEADERSHIP POTENTIAL

I mentioned before that everything rises and falls on leadership. That's true because a person's ability to make things happen in and through others depends entirely on her ability to lead them. Without leadership, there is no teamwork, and people go their own way. That's why today we are going to look at qualities that deal with relating to and leading other people.

PEOPLE TO TAKE ON THE TRIP

3. PEOPLE WHO INFLUENCE OTHERS

If your dream is big and will require the teamwork of a group of people, then any potential leaders you select to go with you on the journey will need to be people of influence. After all, that's what leadership is—influence. And when you think about it, all leaders have two things in common: they're going somewhere, and they're able to persuade others to go with them.

As you look at the people around you, consider the following:

- *Who influences them?* You can tell a lot about *whom* they will influence and *how* they will go about doing it by knowing who their heroes and mentors are.

- *Whom do they influence?* You'll be able to judge their current level of leadership effectiveness by whom they influence.

- *Is their influence increasing or decreasing?* You can tell whether a person is a *past* leader or a *potential* leader by examining which direction the level of influence is going.

To be a good judge of potential leaders, don't just see the person—see all the people that person influences. The greater the influence, the greater the leadership potential and the ability to get others to work with you to accomplish your dream.

List the names of three people you know who influence others, and next to their names, list the people they influence.

Person of Influence	*The People They Influence*
_____	_____
_____	_____
_____	_____

4. PEOPLE WHO ADD VALUE

Every person around you has an effect on you and your ability to fulfill your vision. You've probably noticed this before. Some people seem to hinder you, always taking more from you than they give in return. Others add value to you, improving everything you do. When they come alongside you, synergy develops that takes both of you to a new level.

There are probably people in your life with whom you experience synergy. You inspire and take each other to greater achievement. Can you think of anybody better to take on the success journey? Not only would they help you go far, but also they would make the journey more fun.

List the names of some people with whom you experience synergy.

_____	_____
_____	_____
_____	_____

5. PEOPLE WHO ATTRACT OTHER LEADERS

As you look for potential leaders to take with you on the success journey, you need to realize that there are really two kinds of leaders: those who attract followers and those who attract other leaders. People who attract and team up only with followers will never be able to do anything beyond what they can personally touch or supervise. For each person they interact with, they're influencing only one person—a follower. But people who attract leaders influence many other people through their interaction. Their team can be incredible, especially if the leaders they recruit also attract other leaders.

Besides the obvious factor of influence, there are other significant differences between people who attract followers and people who attract leaders. Here are a few:

Leaders Who Attract Followers . . .	Leaders Who Attract Leaders . . .
Need to be needed.	Want to be succeeded.
Want recognition.	Want to reproduce themselves.
Focus on others' weaknesses.	Focus on others' strengths.
Want to hold on to power.	Want to share power.
Spend their time with others.	Invest their time in others.
Are good leaders.	Are great leaders.
Experience some success.	Experience incredible success.

List the names of a few people you know who attract other leaders.

_____   _____

_____   _____

_____   _____

6. PEOPLE WHO EQUIP OTHERS

It's one thing to attract other people to you and have them join you on the success journey. It's another to equip them with a road map for the trip. The best people always give others more than an invitation—they provide the means to get them there.

Think about this as you search for potential leaders: A person with charisma alone can draw others to her, yet she may not be able to get them to go on the success journey. A leader who is an equipper, however, can empower an army of successful people capable of going anywhere and accomplishing almost anything. As Harvey Firestone said, "It is only as we develop others that we permanently succeed."

List the names of a few people you know who not only attract others, but who also equip others.

_____   _____
_____   _____
_____   _____

TAKE ACTION

As you look for people to join you on the journey, look for leaders who attract other leaders. They will be able to multiply your success. But also know this: In the long run, you can lead only people whose leadership ability is less than or equal to your own. To keep attracting better and better leaders, you will have to keep developing your own leadership ability. In that way, you and your team will continue growing not only in potential, but also in effectiveness. Put yourself to the test. Rate yourself on the following (1=low, 10=high):

Do I influence others? _____
Do I add value to them? _____
Am I attracting other leaders? _____
Am I equipping the people I attract? _____

If you find that you aren't quite at the level that you would like to be at in one of these areas, then start working on that leadership quality. Find resources or mentors who can help you to grow as a leader.

DAY 4

SOMEONE TO COUNT ON

Today we will finish up the list of qualities you'll use to identify the people you want to take with you on the success journey.

PEOPLE TO TAKE ON THE TRIP

7. PEOPLE WHO PROVIDE INSPIRING IDEAS

Nineteenth-century author-playwright Victor Hugo observed, "There's nothing more powerful than an idea whose time has come." Ideas are the greatest resource a successful person could ever have. And when you surround yourself with creative people, you're never at a loss for inspiring ideas.

If you and the people around you continually generate good ideas, all of you have a better opportunity to reach your potential. According to Art Cornwell, author of *Freeing the Corporate Mind: How to Spur Innovation in Business,* creative thinking is what generates ideas. And the better you understand how to generate ideas, the better off you'll be. He suggests:

- The only truly bad ideas are those that die without giving rise to other ideas.

- If you want good ideas, you need a lot of ideas.

- It doesn't matter if "it ain't broke." It probably still can use fixing.

- Great ideas are nothing more than the restructuring of what you already know.

- When all your ideas are added together, the sum should represent your breakthroughs.

You are capable of generating good ideas—probably better able than you think. But you can never have too many ideas. That would be like saying you have too big a budget or too many resources when you're working on a project. That's why you would do well to get people around you who will continue to inspire you with their ideas. And when you find someone with whom you have natural chemistry, the kind that inspires each of you to greatness, you'll find that you always have more ideas than time to carry them out.

List the names of some people you know who generate ideas and contribute to your creativity.

_____ _____

_____ _____

_____ _____

_____ _____

8. PEOPLE WHO POSSESS UNCOMMONLY POSITIVE ATTITUDES
You already know how important a good attitude is to your success. It determines how far you will be able to go on the success journey. But don't underestimate the importance of a positive attitude in the people around you either. When you travel with others, you can go only as fast as the slowest person and as far as the weakest one. Having people around you with negative attitudes is like running a race with a ball and chain on your ankle. You may be able to run for a while, but you're going to get tired fast, and you certainly won't be able to run as far as you'd like.

List the names of a few people you know who display uncommonly positive attitudes.

_____ _____

_____ _____

_____ _____

_____ _____

9. PEOPLE WHO LIVE UP TO THEIR COMMITMENTS

It's been said that commitment is another name for success. And that's really true. Newsman Walter Cronkite declared, "I can't imagine a person becoming a success who doesn't give this game of life everything he's got."

Commitment takes a person to a whole new level when it comes to success. Look at the advantages of commitment as described by motivational speaker Joe Griffith:

> You cannot keep a committed person from success. Place stumbling blocks in his way, and he takes them for stepping-stones, and on them he will climb to greatness. Take away his money, and he makes spurs of his poverty to urge him on. The person who succeeds has a program; he fixes his course and adheres to it; he lays his plans and executes them; he goes straight to his goal. He is not pushed this side and that every time a difficulty is thrust in his way. If he can't go over it, he goes through it.

When the people on your team share your level of commitment, success is inevitable. Commitment helps you overcome obstacles and continue moving forward on the success journey, no matter how tough the going gets. It is the key to success in every aspect of life—marriage, business, personal development, hobbies, sports—you name it. Commitment can carry you a very long way.

List the names of some people you know who live up to their commitments.

_____	_____
_____	_____
_____	_____
_____	_____

10. PEOPLE WHO ARE LOYAL

The last quality you should look for in people to join you on your journey is loyalty. Although this alone does not ensure success in another person, a lack of loyalty is sure to ruin your relationship with him. Think of it this way: when you're looking for potential leaders, if someone you're considering lacks loyalty, he is disqualified. Don't even consider taking him on the journey with you because in the end, he'll hurt you more than help you.

So what does it mean for others to be loyal to you?

- *They love you unconditionally.* They accept you with your strengths and weaknesses intact. They genuinely care for you, not just for what you can do for them. And they are neither trying to make you into someone you're not nor putting you on a pedestal.

- *They represent you well to others.* Loyal people always paint a positive picture of you with others. They may take you to task privately or hold you accountable, but they never criticize you to others.

- *They are able to laugh and cry with you as you travel together.* Loyal people are willing and able to share your joys and sorrows. They make the trip less lonely.

- *They make your dream their dream.* Some people will undoubtedly share the journey with you only briefly. You help one another for a while and then go your separate ways. But a few—a special few—will want to come alongside you and help you for the rest of the journey. These people make your dream their dream. They will be loyal unto death, and when they combine that loyalty with other talents and abilities, they can be some of your most valuable assets. If you find people like that, take good care of them.

The funny thing about loyalty is that the farther you go on the success journey, the more of an issue it becomes. About twenty years ago, my friend Tom Phillippe told me that there would come a time when loyalty in others would become an issue for me. He said, "John, as you become more successful, you will continually ask yourself, *Whom can I trust?*" At the time, I thought he was a terrible cynic, and I told him so. My tendency has always been to trust people and expect the best of them. And I still desire to do that. But Tom's advice has been partly true. I've come to realize that loyalty is a quality to be sought out and valued in the people around me. As you take the success journey, you will probably do the same.

TAKE ACTION

Review the names you listed after each of the ten qualities. What names were repeated the most? Write them below. Pick the top one to three people. These are the best candidates to take on the success journey with you. Set up a time to talk with each person and invite him to join you on the journey. (Look back at Week 2 for ways to express your dream to them.)

1. _____
2. _____
3. _____

DAY 5

CHOOSING THE TEAM

I've been very fortunate as I've traveled on the success journey. Not only have I had wonderful people come alongside me and take the journey with me, but I've also had others take me along when I couldn't make it on my own. A person who has done that is my brother, Larry, one of my favorite people in the whole world. Larry is two and a half years older than I am, and as a kid growing up, I always wanted to tag along with him everywhere he went. I especially loved playing football, baseball, and basketball with him and his friends. Larry was always a team captain because he was a good athlete and leader. And it really meant something to me when he picked me to be on his team instead of letting me be the leftover kid, the last choice, even though I was younger and smaller than anyone else in the group. Larry did that kind of thing for me the whole time I was growing up. But he also included me as we got older, and it meant even more to me.

When Margaret and I were first starting out together, we didn't have much financially. My first full-time position after we got married paid only eighty dollars a month. To help make ends meet, Margaret taught school, and she also cleaned houses and worked in a jewelry store on weekends. We didn't have much, but we were able (just barely) to pay our bills and keep our Volkswagen Beetle running.

We lived like that for the first three years we were married, and as much as I would have liked to take Margaret on vacations every year, it was out of the question. We were skimping on everything just to make it. Putting away extra money to travel was impossible.

Despite that, we were able to take a vacation every one of those three years—thanks to Larry. I still remember when he called us. It was in 1970.

"John, what are you and Margaret going to do this year for vacation?" he asked.

"Well," I answered, "we're just going to stay around here. We've got some things we need to do around the house. And maybe we'll drive to Circleville to see Mom and Dad."

"That's what I thought," said Larry. "Anita and I have made reservations to fly to Acapulco for a week—for four. We want you and Margaret to come along with us."

Larry was doing well financially. He had always had a natural knack for business, and by the time he graduated from college, he was already well on his way to financial independence as the result of some skillful real estate purchases.

"We won't take no for an answer," he said.

Margaret and I didn't have any trouble accepting their offer. We loved both of them dearly, and we were grateful that they wanted to share their vacation time with us. And our trip to Acapulco was incredible, beyond anything we could have imagined. We were in a beautiful, first-class hotel with a view of the ocean. The hotel must have had five pools. The landscape was lush. The food was fabulous. It all seemed very exotic to us. Margaret and I still think back on that as one of our best vacations.

Fortunately, I no longer have to depend on Larry's generosity, but he and I continue to do things together. We've made it our goal to go together to sporting events, such as the Super Bowl, Wimbledon, the World Series, and the best bowl games in college football. We've also committed to playing the top ten golf courses in the world together. And so far, we've made it to about half of them.

Larry and I are brothers, but we don't do things together for that reason. We're taking the success journey together because we want to, and we've decided that it's important to us. And that's what you need to do. You need to decide whom you're going to take with you on the success journey. If you commit yourself to including others, you won't believe the difference it will make in your life—and theirs.

CHARTING THE COURSE

Turn to "My Road Map for Success" in the back of the workbook and complete Section B under *Sowing Seeds That Benefit Others.*

Week

10

WHAT SHOULD WE DO ALONG THE WAY?

DAY 1
Take Somebody with You

DAY 2
Why Many Don't Take Anyone Along

DAY 3
What You Need to Know as You Start

DAY 4
How to Take Others for a Life-Changing Ride

DAY 5
Changing Lives for the Better

PRINCIPAL QUESTIONS

Day 1: What can I learn from those who have mentored me?

Day 2: Is anything holding me back from mentoring someone else?

Day 3: How prepared am I to equip others?

Day 4: What is my plan for equipping someone else?

Day 5: How can I continue on the success journey for years to come?

DAY 1

TAKE SOMEBODY WITH YOU

Have you ever read a book that changed your life, one that revolutionized your thinking and altered how you live in a significant way? I have. In fact, there have been several. But the one that stands out most in my mind is a book I read in 1970 by Dr. Elmer Towns called *The Ten Fastest-Growing Sunday Schools in America*. It was written for people in my profession, and it fueled my dreams and inspired me to dedicate myself to becoming better than I was. And it really propelled me in the direction my life was to take. Little did I know then that my journey and destiny would be linked with those of the book's author, Elmer Towns.

In 1975, I heard about a conference in Waterloo, Iowa, where Elmer was going to speak, and I jumped at the chance to go. I tried to talk with him several times during the breaks so that I could tell him about the enormous influence he had on my life, but each time I tried there was a mob of people around him, and I just couldn't get close to him.

After the conference was over, I went to a Howard Johnson's restaurant to eat lunch, and I had just sat down when who should walk in but Elmer Towns. I introduced myself to him as he came by, and he said, "Come sit with us so that we can get to know each other a little bit."

So there I was, sitting at the table with one of my heroes. I couldn't eat a bite of my lunch; I was so excited I couldn't seem to swallow. And I was thrilled when he suggested that I change my travel times so that I could take the same flight with him to Chicago and sit with him and talk. We got to know each other a little that day, and it was a wonderful experience.

A year later, as I prepared to host my first conference, I decided that I had to have Elmer as one of the speakers. So I called him up and invited him and, to my delight, he said yes. Not only did he come and speak at the conference, but also he spent time with me, casting vision for my life, challenging me to grow, and sharing his insight and wisdom.

Over the years, Elmer has been a mentor and friend, and he has inspired me to be a good leader. A few years ago, I had a chance to honor him publicly by sharing what he has meant to me with a thousand people at a banquet following one of my conferences. And for the occasion, I gave him a gift.

Elmer and I both collect signatures of great leaders. I have signed letters from about a dozen presidents and several clergymen, such as my hero John Wesley. Margaret gets them beautifully framed for me, and I keep them on display. Not long ago I found and purchased an outline of a sermon written by nineteenth-century preacher C. H. Spurgeon. It was a remarkable find. The sermon used as its text the passage from the Bible that says, "Stir up the gift of God, which is in thee" (2 Tim. 1:6 KJV). It's a passage written by the apostle Paul to his protégé, Timothy, encouraging him to use his gifts and pursue his destiny.

I had the Spurgeon sermon only a few months when I realized that I wanted to give it to Elmer at the banquet. Margaret asked me more than once, "Are you sure, John? You may never find another Spurgeon." But I knew it was the right thing to do. I wanted to honor Elmer and give him a gift of appreciation for all he had done, and I couldn't think of a better choice. Elmer loves Spurgeon, and the text from Paul to Timothy perfectly described what Elmer had done for me. He had encouraged me to stir up the gift God had given me. So at the banquet, it was a real thrill to tell all those people about the wonderful things Elmer had done to mentor me over the years and to thank him with that gift.

What Elmer did with me, I have tried to pass on to others. I've already spent a good part of my life teaching and mentoring others in the areas of leadership, personal growth, spiritual development, and success. And I have dedicated the rest of my time on earth to continuing to do that. So the answer to the question that is the title of this week's studies, "What should we do along the way?" is this: Take somebody with you. It's not enough for you to finish the race. To really be successful, you need to take somebody with you across the finish line. Henry Ford maintained, "Most people think of it [success] in terms of getting. Success, however, begins in terms of giving."[1]

TAKE ACTION

Think about someone who has been a mentor to you. What did he do to influence and inspire you on your success journey?

_____

_____

_____

If possible, meet with this person to say thank you and to discuss ways you can inspire someone else on his success journey.

WHY MANY DON'T TAKE ANYONE ALONG

Most people who desire success focus almost entirely on themselves, not others, when they start to make the journey. They usually think in terms of what they can get—in position, power, prestige, money, and similar perks. But that's not the way to become truly successful. To do that, you have to give to others. As Douglas M. Lawson said, "We exist temporarily through what we take, but we live forever through what we give."

That's why it's so essential to focus on raising others to a higher level. And we can do that with people from every area of our lives: at work and home, in church and the clubhouse. That's evidently what Texas Representative Wright Patman did, according to a story told by Senator Paul Simon. He said that Patman died at age eighty-two while serving in the U.S. House of Representatives. At his funeral, an older woman who lived in his district was heard to have said, "He rose up mighty high, but he brung us all up with him."

> *Do you have a history of raising others to a higher level? If so, describe how.*

_____

_____

_____

_____

If mentoring others is such a rewarding calling, why doesn't everyone do it? One reason is that it takes work. But there are also many others. Here are a few of the most common ones.

PEOPLE DON'T MENTOR BECAUSE OF . . .

INSECURITY

Virginia Arcastle commented, "When people are made to feel secure and important and appreciated, it will no longer be necessary for them to whittle down others in order to seem bigger in comparison." That's what insecure people tend to do: make themselves look better at others' expense.

Truly successful people, on the other hand, raise others up. And they don't feel threatened by the thought of having others become more successful and move to a higher level. They are growing and striving for their potential; they aren't worried about having someone replace them. They're nothing like the executive who wrote a memo to the personnel director saying, "Search the organization for an alert, aggressive young man who could step into my shoes—and when you find him, fire him." Raising up others is a successful person's joy.

What insecurities must you overcome? How will you do it?

_____

_____

_____

EGO

Some people's egos are so huge that they have to be either the bride at the wedding or the corpse at the funeral. They think other people exist only to serve them in some way or another. Adolf Hitler was like that. According to Robert Waite, when Hitler was searching for a chauffeur, he interviewed thirty candidates for the job. He selected the shortest man in the group and kept him as his personal driver for the rest of his life, even though the man required special blocks under the driver's seat so that he could see over the steering wheel.[2] Hitler used others to make himself appear bigger and better than he really was. A person consumed with himself never considers spending time raising others up.

In what ways must you get over yourself in order to better help others? How do you raise others up? List the positive comments you've made about others or actions you have taken to benefit someone other than yourself today.

_____

_____

_____

AN INABILITY TO DISCERN PEOPLE'S "SUCCESS SEEDS"

I believe every person has the seed of success inside. Too many people can't find it in themselves, let alone in others, and as a result, they don't reach their potential. But many do find that seed, and chances are, you are one of those people. The good news is that once you are able to find it in yourself, you're better able to do the same with others. When you do, it benefits both of you because you and the person you help will be able to fulfill the purposes for which each was born.

The ability to find another's seed of success takes commitment, diligence, and a genuine desire to focus on others. You have to look at the person's gifts, temperament, passions, successes, joys, and opportunities. And once you find that seed, you need to fertilize it with encouragement and water it with opportunity. If you do, the person will blossom before your eyes.

List the names of two people with whom you work. Next to their names list the seeds of success, the positive qualities that they possess, which you will begin to focus on when working with them and speaking of them to others.

Person   *Seeds of Success*

_____   _____

_____   _____

A WRONG CONCEPT OF SUCCESS

The average person doesn't know what you know about success—that it is knowing your purpose, growing to reach your maximum potential, and sowing seeds to benefit others. He is scrambling to arrive at a destination or to acquire more possessions than the next-door neighbors own.

But you know that success is a journey, and the most you can hope for is to do your best with what you've got.

Fred Smith said: "Some of us tend to think, *I could have been a success . . . but I never had the opportunity. I wasn't born into the right family,* or *I didn't have the money to go to the best school.* But when we measure success by the extent we're using what we've received, it eliminates that frustration." And one of the most vital aspects of how we're using what we received comes in the area of helping others. As Cullen Hightower remarked, "A true measure of your worth includes all the benefits others have gained from your success."

How can you share your definition of success with others to help them on their own success journey?

_____

_____

_____

A LACK OF TRAINING

The final reason many people don't raise up the people around them is that they don't know how to do it. Equipping others isn't something most people learn in school. Even if you went to college to become a teacher, you were probably trained to disseminate information to a group, not to come alongside a single person, pour into her life, and raise her to a higher level.

TAKE ACTION

Add at least one resource to your personal growth plan that will help you to learn how to develop and equip other people. List the title of that resource below. (If you are having a difficult time finding resources, visit The INJOY Group's web site www.injoy.com.)

_____

DAY 3

WHAT YOU NEED TO KNOW AS YOU START

Raising people to a higher level and helping them be successful involves more than giving them information or skills. If that were the case, every new employee would go from trainee to success as soon as he understood how to do his job; every child would be successful whenever she learned something new at school. But success doesn't automatically follow knowledge. The process is complicated because you're working with people. Understanding some basic concepts about people opens the door to your ability to develop others. For example, remind yourself that:

EVERYONE WANTS TO FEEL WORTHWHILE

Donald Laird said, "Always help people increase their own self-esteem. Develop your skill in making other people feel important. There is hardly a higher compliment you can pay an individual than helping him be useful and to find satisfaction from his usefulness." When a person doesn't feel good about himself, he will never believe he is successful, no matter what he accomplishes. But a person who feels worthwhile is ripe for success.

How can you make others feel worthwhile?

_____

_____

EVERYONE NEEDS AND RESPONDS TO ENCOURAGEMENT

One of my favorite quotes comes from industrialist Charles Schwab, who said, "I have yet to find the man, however exalted his station, who did not do better work and put forth greater effort under a spirit of approval than under a spirit of criticism." If you desire to raise up another person, then you need to become one of her staunchest supporters. People can tell when you don't believe in them.

How can you show people that you believe in them?

_____

_____

PEOPLE ARE NATURALLY MOTIVATED

I've found that people are naturally motivated. If you doubt that, just watch toddlers soon after they learn to walk. They're into everything. They have natural curiosity, and you can't get them to stay still. I believe that innate sense of motivation continues to exist in adults, but for too many people it has been beaten down by lack of support, busyness, stress, bad attitudes, lack of appreciation, scarce resources, poor training, or faulty communication. To get people excited about growing to their potential, you need to remotivate them. Once you help them overcome the old things that knocked them down, they often motivate themselves.

How can you help to restore people's confidence in themselves?

_____

_____

PEOPLE BUY INTO THE PERSON BEFORE BUYING INTO HIS LEADERSHIP

Many unsuccessful people who try to lead others have the mistaken belief that people will follow them because their cause is good. But that's not the way leadership works. People will follow you only when they believe in you. That principle applies even when you're offering to develop other people and raise them to a higher level.

Describe people's belief in you.

_____

_____

The more you understand people, the greater your chance of success in mentoring. And if you have highly developed people skills and genuinely care about others, the process will probably come to you naturally.

TAKE ACTION

Find one person to concentrate on today. Invest in this person by helping him or her to feel worthwhile, by being encouraging and building his confidence.

What actions can you take to do this?

_____

_____

_____

What words can you say to reinforce your confidence in this person?

_____

_____

_____

DAY 4

HOW TO TAKE OTHERS FOR A LIFE-CHANGING RIDE

Whether you have a gift for interacting positively with people or you have to really work at it, you are capable of mentoring others and lifting them to a higher level. You can help them develop a Road Map for Success and go on the success journey with you as long as you keep growing as a person and as a leader.

Over the next two days we will look at the steps you will need to take in order to take people for a ride—one that will change their lives forever.

PEOPLE DEVELOPMENT: HOW AND WHY

MAKE PEOPLE DEVELOPMENT YOUR TOP PRIORITY

If you want to succeed in developing people, you have to make it a top priority. It's always easier to dismiss people than to develop them. If you don't believe it, just ask any employer or divorce attorney. But many people don't realize that while dismissing others is easy, it also has a high price. In business, the costs come from lost productivity, administrative costs of firing and hiring, and low morale. In marriage, the cost is often broken lives.

I learned this lesson when I was in my first pastorate. My desire was to build a large church. If I did, I thought I would be a success. And I accomplished that goal. I took that small congregation from three people to more than 250, and I did it in a tiny, rural community. But I did the whole thing myself—with Margaret's help. I didn't develop anyone else. As a result, we had success only in the places I touched; we had complaints in all the places I didn't touch; and everything fell apart after I left. I succeeded, but only for a moment. And I didn't bring lasting success to anyone else.

I learned a lot from that experience, and in my second position, I made it a priority to develop others. Over an eight-year period, I developed thirty-five people, and they built up that church and made it successful. And after I left, the church was just as successful as when I was there because those other leaders were able to carry on without me. If you want to make a difference in the lives of others, do the same. Commit yourself to developing people and taking them on the trip with you.

How are you showing your commitment to developing people in your everyday actions?

_____

_____

LIMIT WHOM YOU TAKE ALONG

Like it or not, you can't take everyone along with you on the success journey. As you begin to develop people, think of the journey as being similar to a trip in a small, private plane. If you try to take too many people along, you'll never get off the ground. Besides, your time is limited, and it makes more sense to help a few learn how to fly and reach their potential than to show a big group only enough to whet their appetites.

When I teach leadership seminars, I always teach what's known as the Pareto (80/20) Principle. In a nutshell, it says that if you focus your attention on the top 20 percent in anything you do, you will get an 80 percent return. In the case of developing people, you should spend 80 percent of your time developing only the top 20 percent of the people around you. That would include the most important people in your life, such as your family, and the people who have the most potential. If you try to mentor and develop more people than that, you're going to spread yourself too thin.

How does your calendar reflect the 80/20 Principle? (If it doesn't, how can you change it so that it does?)

_____

_____

DEVELOP RELATIONSHIPS BEFORE STARTING OUT

Mentors make the common mistake of trying to lead others before developing relationships with them. Look around you, and you can see it happening all the time. A new manager starts with a company and expects the people working there to respond to her authority without question. A coach asks his players to trust him and go to the mat for him when they don't even know one another. A divorced father who hasn't seen his children in several years reinitiates contact with them and expects them to respond to him automatically, even though they haven't had time to get reacquainted and comfortable with each other. In each of these instances, the leader is expecting to make an impact on the people before building the relationship. The followers may comply with what the leader's position requires, but they'll never go beyond that.

The best leaders understand the important role of relationships when it comes to success. For example, Lee Iacocca once asked legendary Green Bay Packer Coach Vince Lombardi what it took to make a winning team. Here's what Lombardi answered:

> There are a lot of coaches with good ball clubs who know the fundamentals and have plenty of discipline but still don't win the game. Then you come to the third ingredient: if you're going to play together as a team, you've got to care for one another. You've got to love each other. Each player has to be thinking about the next guy and saying to himself: "If I don't block that man, Paul is going to get his legs broken. I have to do my job well in order that he can do his." The difference between mediocrity and greatness is the feeling these guys have for each other.[3]

And that concept doesn't apply only to football. It also applies to individuals traveling together on the success journey. If the relationships aren't there first, people won't travel far with one another.

One advantage to building relationships with people before starting on the journey together is that you find out what kind of "traveling companions" you're going to have. If you've ever gone on a trip with someone you ended up disliking, then you know what a difficult situation that can be.

As you bring others alongside you for the success journey, choose people you expect to like. Then get to know them to verify your choice. It's the best way to be effective—and enjoy the trip.

How can you develop better relationships with the people you are going to equip?

_____

_____

GIVE HELP UNCONDITIONALLY

When you start developing people, you should never go into it with the idea of getting something out of it. That attitude will almost certainly backfire on you. If you expect to get something in return and you don't, you will become bitter. And if you get back less than you expect, you'll resent the time you spent. No, you have to go into the process expecting nothing. Give for the sake of giving—just for the joy of seeing another person learn to fly. When you approach it that way, your attitude will always remain positive. And the times you do get something in return, it's a wonderful win-win situation.

Be honest with yourself: Are you helping others for their benefit or yours? If your motives are selfish, how can you change?

_____

_____

_____

LET THEM FLY WITH YOU FOR A WHILE

I want to share a secret with you. It guarantees success in mentoring. Are you ready? Here it is: *Never work alone.* I know that sounds too simple, but it is truly the secret to developing others. Whenever you do anything that you want to pass along to others, take someone with you.

This isn't necessarily a natural practice for many of us. The learning model that most people use in America for teaching others is one the Greeks passed down to us. It's a cognitive "classroom" approach, like the one used by Socrates to teach Plato, and Plato to teach Aristotle. The leader stands and speaks, asking questions or lecturing. The follower sits at his feet, listening. His goal is to comprehend the instructor's ideas.

But that's not the only model available for developing others. We also have one used by another ancient culture: the Hebrews. Their method was more like on-the-job training. It was built on relationships and common experience. It's what craftspeople have done for centuries. They take apprentices who work alongside them until they master their craft and are able to pass it along to others. Their model looks something like this:

- *I do it.* First I learn to do the job. I have to understand the why as well as the how, and I try to perfect my craft.

- *I do it—and you watch.* I demonstrate it while you observe, and during the process, I explain what I'm doing and why.

- *You do it—and I watch.* As soon as possible, we exchange roles. I give you permission and authority to take over the job, but I stay with you to offer advice, correction, and encouragement.

- *You do it.* Once you're proficient, I step back and let you work alone. The learner has risen to a higher level. And as soon as he is on that higher level, the teacher is free to move on to higher things.

In all the years I've been equipping and developing others, I've never found a better way to do it than this. And for a long time, whenever I got ready to perform one of my duties, I made it a practice to take along the person I wanted to equip for the task. Before we did it, we talked about what was going to happen. And afterward, we'd discuss what we did.

How can you use the model I've described with the person you are equipping?

_____

_____

PUT FUEL IN THEIR TANKS

People won't get far without fuel—and that means resources for their continuing personal growth. Any mentor can give that valuable gift to someone he is developing. Many people don't know where to find good resources or what kinds of materials to select, especially when they're just starting out.

I regularly share books, tapes, and videos with the people I'm developing and equipping. I also enjoy sending them to seminars. My goal is always to "bring something to the table" when I spend time with someone, whether it's an employee, a colleague, or a friend. I always want to be a resource person for them.

You can do the same thing for others. Start by sharing the books and tapes that have changed your life. And be on the lookout for good material in the other person's areas of interest. There are few greater thrills than putting into others' hands a resource that can help take them to the next level.

TAKE ACTION

As you prepare to develop other people, take time to get to know them better. Ask them to share their stories with you—their journeys so far. Find out what makes them tick, their strengths and weaknesses, their temperaments. And spend some time with them outside the environment where you typically see them. If you work together, then play sports together. If you know each other from church, meet with them at their workplace. If you go to school together, then spend some time together at home. You can even use this principle with your family. For example, if you spend time with your children outside your everyday environment, you'll learn a lot more about them. It will develop your relationship in ways it hasn't before, and it will help you grow.

DAY 5

CHANGING LIVES FOR THE BETTER

With people development as your top priority, you are now reaching for a whole new level of success on your journey. And today we will finish up with the last three steps on how to take people on a ride that will change their lives, and yours, forever.

PEOPLE DEVELOPMENT: HOW AND WHY

STAY WITH THEM UNTIL THEY CAN SOLO SUCCESSFULLY

I've been told that every student pilot looks forward to the first solo flight with anticipation—and a certain amount of fear. But a good flight instructor wouldn't allow a student to take that solo flight until he is ready, nor would he let a student avoid her solo once she is ready. I guess you could say that's the difference between a true mentor and a wanna-be. It's kind of like the difference between a flight instructor and a travel agent. The one stays with you, guiding you through the entire process until you're ready to fly. The other hands you a ticket and says, "Have a good flight."

As you develop people, remember that you are taking them on the success journey with you, not sending them. Stay with them until they're ready to fly. And when they are ready, get them on their way.

How will you determine when someone is ready to fly on his own?

_____

_____

_____

_____

CLEAR THE FLIGHT PATH

Even after teaching people to fly, providing them with fuel, and giving them permission to take the controls, some mentors don't take the last step required to make their people successful.

They don't give them an unencumbered flight path. They usually don't intentionally restrict the people they're developing, but it still happens.

Here are five common obstacles mentors create for potential leaders:

1. *Lack of clear direction:* Many times a potential leader gets mentored and learns how to do a job, then he is left adrift, without any direction from his leader.

2. *Bureaucracy:* She learns how her leader works and thinks, and then she is put into a bureaucratic system that stifles the innovative spirit that the mentor just engendered.

3. *Isolation:* Everyone needs a community of people with whom to share and from whom to draw support. Often if the mentor doesn't provide it, the new leader won't have it.

4. *Busywork:* Work with no perceived value demoralizes and demotivates people.

5. *Poor or dishonest communication:* An agenda that isn't communicated honestly to the person being developed hinders the relationship and confuses the potential leader.

Once you begin to develop others, check to see that you're not leaving obstacles in their path. Give them clear direction, positive support, and the freedom to fly. What you do can make the difference between their failure and success. And when they succeed, so do you.

How can you give the people you're developing a clear flight path when they are ready? Which of the five common obstacles might be hindering the people you're trying to help?

_____

_____

_____

_____

HELP THEM REPEAT THE PROCESS

After you've done everything you can to help your people, and they have taken off and are soaring, you may think you're finished. But you're not. There is still one more step you must take to complete the process. You have to help them learn to repeat the development process and teach others to fly. You see, there is no success without a successor.

A great joy in my life has been to see how leaders I've developed and equipped have turned around and repeated the process with others. It must be similar to the joy a great-grandfather feels as he looks at the generations that have been raised up in his family. With each generation, the success continues.

The most remarkable example of equipping in my life has definitely been Dan Reiland, who was my executive pastor for many years. During the first eight years he worked for me, I spent a great deal of time developing him. Then for the next six years, he took over the responsibility of mentoring and equipping my entire staff. In addition, he has also personally developed more than one hundred people on his own. And now some of those people, such as Glenn Finch and Don Moser, are continuing the process by producing yet another generation of successful leaders.

The positive effects of developing others are remarkable. But you don't have to be a remarkable or unusually talented person to mentor others. You can raise up people around you and teach them to fly, just as I have. It does take desire and a commitment to the process, but it is the most rewarding part of success. Raising up others is the greatest joy in the world. You see, once people learn to fly, they're capable of going just about anywhere. And sometimes when they're flying high, they help you along too.

Your goal as you take the success journey should be to help others stretch and grow. Take others with you and help them change their lives for the better. Nothing in life is more fun—or has a greater return. You'll never regret the time you invest in people.

CHARTING THE COURSE

One last time, turn to "My Road Map for Success" in the back of the workbook and complete Section C under *Sowing Seeds That Benefit Others.*

Also, mark a date on your calendar, six months from today, to review your "Road Map for Success."

NOTES

WEEK 1
1. Ecclesiastes 5:10 NIV.
2. Bill Rose, *New York Herald Tribune,* 8 November 1948.

WEEK 2
1. Florence Littauer, *Silver Boxes* (Dallas: Word, 1989), 136–38, 146–47.

WEEK 3
1. Nell Mohney, "Beliefs Can Influence Attitudes," *Kingsport Times-News,* 25 July 1986, 4B.
2. *Cox Report on American Business,* 1983.
3. Donald Robinson, "Mind Over Disease," *Reader's Digest.*

WEEK 4
1. Bob Buford, *Halftime* (Grand Rapids: Zondervan, 1994), 122.
2. "Put Your Purpose on Paper," *Discipleship Journal,* September/October 1992, 77–78.
3. *New Attitude,* Spring 1995.

WEEK 5
1. John C. Maxwell, *Breakthrough Parenting* (Colorado Springs: Focus on the Family, 1996), 116.
2. Denis E. Waitley and Robert B. Tucker, *Winning the Innovation Game* (Grand Rapids: Revell, 1986).

WEEK 6
1. Denis Waitley, *Seeds of Greatness* (Grand Rapids: Revell, 1983).
2. *Leaders on Leadership: Interviews with Top Executives* (Boston: Harvard Business, 1992).

WEEK 7
1. Bob Buford, *Halftime* (Grand Rapids: Zondervan, 1994), 30, 164.
2. Bud Greenspan, *The 100 Greatest Moments in Olympic History.*

WEEK 8
1. Gary Bauer, "American Family Life," *Focus on the Family,* July 1994, 2.
2. Florence Littauer, *Personality Plus* (Grand Rapids: Revell, 1983), 24–81.

3. Thomas Armstrong, 7 *Kinds of Smart: Identifying and Developing Your Many Intelligences* (New York: Plume, 1993), 9–11.
4. William Kilpatrick, *Why Johnny Can't Tell Right from Wrong.*

WEEK 10

1. Quoted in Tim Hansel, *When I Relax I Feel Guilty* (Colorado Springs: Chariot Family, 1979).
2. Robert G. C. Waite, *The Psychopathic God: Adolf Hitler* (New York: Basic Books, 1977), 244–45.
3. Lee Iacocca and William Novak, *Iacocca* (New York: Bantam, 1986).

About the Author

John C. Maxwell, known as America's expert on leadership, is the founder of The INJOY Group™, an organization dedicated to helping people maximize their personal and leadership potential. Through his seminars, books, and tapes, Dr. Maxwell encourages and motivates more than one million people each year. He has authored more than twenty-four books, including *The 17 Indisputable Laws of Teamwork, The 21 Irrefutable Laws of Leadership, Becoming a Person of Influence, The Success Journey, Developing the Leader Within You,* and *Developing the Leaders Around You.*

John C. Maxwell has the tools to equip you on Your Success Journey!

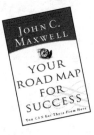

Spend 10 weeks reading *Your Roadmap For Success*. Read one chapter each week and begin to discover your own special talents and abilities that will equip you for your success journey.

Leadership expert John C. Maxwell encourages readers to explore and enhance their own skills. John walks you through the process of evaluating where you are currently and determining where you are going, who you should take with you and how you should handle things along the way.

These principles can be used in any endeavor. No matter who you are, if you learn and apply these insights, your journey will be one of success.

Personal Growth: The Mark of a Continuing Leader
— Video Application Series

This highly practical study will help you become the person you resolve to be every January 1st! And, it will give you the tools to teach the people around you how to reach their maximum potential too!

John Maxwell will share with you:
- 8 simple steps to a lifestyle of personal growth
- 12 keys on how to find good information
- How to create a growth environment
- The 7-point system to apply what you learn

You'll never be the same.

Five Levels of Leadership: The Remarkable Process of Influence
— Video Application Series

Get ready to grow as a leader! This video training series not only explains the five different levels of leadership, but it also will forever alter the way you lead and the reasons why people follow you. John Maxwell takes you through the levels one by one, showing you exactly how to make changes that will increase your influence and results.

Priorities: The Pathway to Success
— Video Application Series

Get more done in less time! One of John's most popular series, these refreshing lectures explain the Pareto Principle — getting 80 percent of your results from 20 percent of your priorities. Maxwell shares sanity-saving ways to get control of your schedule, determine your priorities and make the most of your people, time and money.

Priority Code: RMP

The INJOY Group™
A Lifelong Partner Dedicated to
Lifting Your Potential

The INJOY Group™, founded in 1985 by Dr. John C. Maxwell, dedicates itself to adding value to individuals and organizations across America and around the world. It accomplishes its mission by forging lasting partnerships that foster personal growth and organizational effectiveness.

The INJOY Group™ consists of . . .

INJOY® Resources—Equipping People to Succeed

INJOY® Conferences—Empowering Leaders to Excel

INJOY Stewardship Services®—Energizing Churches to Raise
    Funds for Financing the Future

EQUIP™—Affecting Leadership Development in Emerging
    Countries, American Urban Centers, and Academic
    Communities

Each year, The INJOY Group™ partners with tens of thousands of people, dozens of church denominations, and countless business and nonprofit organizations to help people reach their potential.

To learn more about Dr. John C. Maxwell or any division of The INJOY Group™, visit us at:

www.INJOY.com

Books by Dr. John C. Maxwell
Can Teach You How to Be a REAL Success

RELATIONSHIPS
Be a People Person (Victor Books)
Becoming a Person of Influence (Thomas Nelson)
The Power of Influence (Honor Books)
The Power of Partnership in the Church (J. Countryman)
The Treasure of a Friend (J. Countryman)

EQUIPPING
Developing the Leaders Around You (Thomas Nelson)
Partners in Prayer (Thomas Nelson)
The Success Journey (Thomas Nelson)
Success One Day at a Time (J. Countryman)

ATTITUDE
Be All You Can Be (Victor Books)
Failing Forward (Thomas Nelson)
The Power of Thinking (Honor Books)
Living at the Next Level (Thomas Nelson)
Think On These Things (Beacon Hill)
The Winning Attitude (Thomas Nelson)
Your Bridge to a Better Future (Thomas Nelson)
The Power of Attitude (Honor Books)

LEADERSHIP
The 21 Indispensable Qualities of a Leader (Thomas Nelson)
The 21 Irrefutable Laws of Leadership (Thomas Nelson)
The 21 Most Powerful Minutes in a Leader's Day (Thomas Nelson)
Developing the Leader Within You (Thomas Nelson)
The Power of Leadership (Honor Books)
The 17 Indisputable Laws of Teamwork (Thomas Nelson)
The 17 Essential Qualities of a Team Player (Thomas Nelson, Jan. 2002)

WORKBOOK NOTES

Body for Life Notes

"What are my reasons for deciding to change?
- I want to feel young, with no limitations on what I can do physically
- I want to be physically attractive to Lori and not embarrassed to be in swim trunks
- I want to be able to play and compete with the kids in their sports activities
- I want to be in the best shape of my life at 30 yrs - I can do this!

What are the five most important, specific accomplishments ~~you~~ I need to make, within the next 12 wks, to be pleased with the progress of my body and life?
- Run < 6 min mile for 2 miles (=12min/2mi.)
- Run ½ marathon < 1 hr 45 min
- Bench press (Soloflex) my weight - 165 lbs
- 75 pushups in 2 min
- Hike a 14er w/ a 50 lb pack

Three patterns of action that might prevent me:
(1) Not getting adequate sleep (throws off workouts)
(2) Skipping/down-grading high-intensity workouts
(3) Poor eating habits

↑
UNAUTHORIZED!

At the end of 12 weeks I will...
(By August 11, 2009)

WORKBOOK NOTES

Three new patterns I need to start to achieve my goals:
(1) Get 7hrs of sleep at night, every night
(2) Plan and complete intense workouts
(3) Eat nutritiously, consistently

misfortune is a bridge, not an obstacle. It can provide a way to know or be something beyond what you are. You need to cross it to grow. Most people never get the chance.

• order Accu-Measure @ www.bodytrends.com

WORKBOOK NOTES

WORKBOOK NOTES

WORKBOOK NOTES

WORKBOOK NOTES

WORKBOOK NOTES